For the students, of course.

Put yourself in the student's chair.

Lean University

A Guide to Renewal and Prosperity

Bob Emiliani, Ph.D.

The CLBM, LLC
Wethersfield, Conn.

Lean University: A Guide to Renewal and Prosperity / M.L. "Bob" Emiliani

Cover design and illustrations by Bob Emiliani.

ISBN-13: 978-0-9898631-2-4

Library of Congress Control Number: 2015908483

1. Higher Education 2. Administration 3. Lean Management
4. Leadership 5. Business 6. Non-profit

First Edition: June 2015

Published previously as an e-book titled: *We Can Do It: Improving the Relevancy and Value of Higher Education* (2012). This print version is revised and expanded.

Published by The CLBM, LLC, Wethersfield, Connecticut, USA

Manufactured using digital print-on-demand technology.

CONTENTS

Preface

Progressive Lean management has had an incredibly difficult time since the late 1970s. It has been adopted by nearly all big manufacturers, most of whom proceeded to use Lean narrowly as a tool for short-term cost cutting, layoffs, and outsourcing. Manufacturing company leaders, especially finance executives, have comprehensively misunderstood Lean. As a result, most people who have heard of Lean management have a strong negative opinion of it. It is a reputation well deserved.

The aim of this book is to reverse this impression by giving readers a clear understanding of Lean management. You will learn the intent of Lean management is *not* to do harm; that its actual intent is to develop people and improve processes in mutually beneficial ways that result in prosperity for all. It has been that way from the beginning.

Service organizations have lagged in the adoption of Lean management for 20 or more years. Perhaps they were wise to wait, unintentional though it may have been. These late adopters have the benefit of learning from the mistakes of others, especially manufacturers. They so fouled-up Lean that the lessons learned on what not to do can only be expressed in book after book.

As a result, the practice of Lean management in some service organizations has greatly improved, both for-profit and non-profit.

The time has arrived for university leaders to understand and practice Lean management. While those in higher education think they are different in innumerable ways compared to other service organizations, the fact is they share many more similarities than differences. If they can accept this reality, then Lean management offers a pathway for improving higher education – both academic and administrative processes – that cannot be achieved in any other way.

Leaders of organizations are professionals who should possess an immense knowledge of their chosen field: management. Yet most leaders ignore the over 120-year history progressive management. They act like neutrinos in that they pass through this immense body of dense knowledge without ever interacting with it. As a result, the important problems that most organizations face continue to be addressed using the same tired ideas and methods that harm people.

I hope this book changes that. Maybe it is substantive enough to interact with a few neutrinos and generate a positive reaction – one that leads to change for the better, especially in academic work.

As you read this book, please be attentive to the strategic advantages that Lean management (done right) can impart to organizations that exist in competitive environments.

Finally, I wish to thank my students for all the constructive feedback they have given to me over the years. I could not have improved without them.

Bob Emiliani
2 June 2015
Wethersfield, Conn.

Introduction

The purpose of this book is to introduce the Lean management system to university leaders: trustees, presidents, provosts, senior administrators, deans, managers, department chairs, and supervisors. This book will be useful to departments of higher education, legislators, and governors in the case of public universities. Faculty (full time and part-time), staff, students, alumni, and public and private sector leaders will also find this book valuable and informative. It will help these audiences understand Lean management and recognize it as a preferred means to address current and long-term challenges in higher education.

It must be clearly understood from the outset that Lean management is fully compatible with the successful university traditions of shared governance and academic freedom, and consistent with the interests of all stakeholders, including labor union leaders and their members [1]. Lean is not a means to lay people off or outsource work, nor is it a means to force higher education into a factory model or to corporatize higher education. It is not a path to edutainment or 100 percent graduation rates.

Lean is a management system that can be used by any organization whose leaders are serious about continuous improvement. Its focus is daily problem-solving and improving processes in ways that do not harm key stakeholders.

The challenges in higher education cannot be met using the same old tired routines of budget cutting, consolidating academic and support units, leveraging procurement spend, consolidating information technology, disruptive re-organizations, and so on. These painful, zero-sum (win-lose) approaches to solving problems drive people apart and will not lead to the kinds of substantial or lasting improvements demanded by students and other stakeholders.

They also reflect a dramatic void in creativity and innovative thinking among university leaders.

Lean University provides information that university leaders need to know to correctly begin their practice of Lean management. Specifically, its application in academic processes, which is the source of value creation in higher education. Administrative processes, while not a source of value creation, do shape student's perception of value. They are important processes that can also be greatly improved using Lean principles and practices [2].

This book presents a proven path for improving teaching, individual courses, and academic programs. Lean management provides the means to improve access, affordability, and attainment while also resulting in educational services that have greater relevance and value.

Lean University will hopefully inspire administrators, staff, and faculty to learn a different, better way to improve academics, student engagement and learning, graduation rates, and post-graduation student success (including less student debt), while also improving quality and reducing costs in non-zero-sum (win-win) ways.

Lean is a progressive system of management that differs substantially in almost every way from the conventional management practice that university leaders have long used. This means that university leaders will have to learn many new things, some of which will be difficult [3].

Those that can do so will realize Lean management is a more effective way to improve the value proposition in academics without compromising academic rigor. Demands on students will likely increase, yet they will be much more focused.

Lean management offers the unique opportunity to consistently do good without doing harm, provided the management system is correctly understood and practiced. Historically, this has been a challenge for which most senior managers received a failing grade.

Hence, some advice to readers: If you find yourself saying: "I already know that," don't listen.

Notes

[1] Union leaders have long misunderstood or ignored the Lean management system. They could be great champions and teachers of Lean management if they instead gained a proper understanding of it.

[2] Several universities have been active for a number of years in applying Lean principles and practices to administrative processes. These include: University of Central Oklahoma, Winona State University, Michigan Technological University, Cardiff University, and University of St. Andrews. In most cases, it has been relatively easy to gain support for Lean from university administrators, yet very difficult to gain their participation in continuous improvement activities. Such resistance (or indifference) demonstrates that management's commitment to improvement is far weaker than they would like anyone to believe.

[3] Lean management and six sigma are often mistakenly viewed by managers to be the same or comparable. Lean is a management system, while six sigma is a quality improvement tool useful only under narrow circumstances. The two are not comparable. Lean people would not be interested in six sigma because it requires specialists, and continuous improvement activities will therefore be paced by the capacity of the specialists. With Lean, you want everyone in the organization to be able to identify a problem, determine its root causes, and identify and implement practical countermeasures – not just specialists. Lean and six sigma do not belong together. Most managers face enough of a challenge with Lean management; why make Lean more complicated by adding six sigma?

1

What Is Lean Management?

This chapter seeks to answer to questions: "What is Lean management?" and "Is Lean management bad?" Let's start with the second question.

Progressive management is commonly known today as "Lean management." It is a comprehensive system of management for every part of an organization, from human resources to academics to purchasing, marketing, finance, and facilities. The management system traces its roots to the late 1800s, beginning with the work of Frederick Winslow Taylor and Frank Gilbreth. By 1910, progressive management had developed into a system called "Scientific Management." Almost from the start, there was division between Taylorists, who promoted use of the management system in its entirety, and others who promoted use of only parts of the system with the intent to drive workers harder and achieve short-term financial gains for the company.

The Scientific Management system was widely misunderstood and misapplied by managers unknown, in companies large and small. Yet, it was Taylor who got all the blame when his management system's principles and practices were fouled-up by managers and consultants. As a result, Taylor was asked to testify before Congress for three days in January 1912 to explain Scientific Management.

In defense of his management system and out of frustration for its widespread misuse, Taylor said in testimony to Congress [1]:

> "It ceases to be scientific management
> the moment it is used for bad."

All that Taylor was trying to do was to improve workplace productivity without burning people out and improve cooperation between management and workers, both in a non-zero-sum (win-win) way. These were simple but important goals for the time, yet far from the norm of how business was then conducted. Can Scientific Management be used for bad? Yes it can. But that was not Taylor's intent. It was managers who used Scientific Management with a different intent, one that resulted in bad outcomes for people – especially employees.

Likewise, we must say exactly the same thing about Lean:

> "It ceases to be Lean management the
> moment it is used for bad."

Just as in Taylor's day, Lean has been used in recent times for bad. Managers apply Lean with a different intent: to speed people up, to cut costs, to lay people off, and so on. That is not the intent of Lean management [2].

Progressive management has evolved over the last 120 years and is today substantially different than it was in Taylor's day. Importantly, it has gone from various tools narrowly focused on improving production and non-production efficiency to a human-centered management system designed to be responsive to the needs of all key stakeholders [3].

Progressive Lean management is broadly focused on how to manage all aspects of an enterprise. It has been greatly improved through exceptional contributions made by managers and workers in different companies and industries. Carefully developed over time by management practitioners – not by academics – the focus of Lean management has always been on achieving practical improvements that work in the real world and that are good for people.

In recent years, organizations in a wide variety of service industries, such as healthcare, insurance, finance, state government, and, finally, higher education, have realized the opportunity that progressive Lean management represents. Understood correctly,

Lean can significantly improve management practice and yield better outcomes for all key stakeholders: employees, suppliers, customers (students and payers), investors, and communities. To do this, however, requires changes in leadership practices as well as changes in management practices. Lean management requires the leadership team of an organization to learn many new ways of thinking and doing things. Lean must be led, and to lead effectively the leaders must understand and apply Lean principles and practices daily. University leaders cannot lead an organization practicing Lean management if they do not know it themselves.

Next, let's define Lean Management to ensure a common understanding of key terms. Without this basis of common understanding, Lean management will never prosper in an organization. Variation in people's understanding of Lean has proven to be a significant barrier in its proper application and therefore usually causes harm instead of good. When people misunderstand and misapply Lean, one or more stakeholders suffer. Therefore, it is critical to establish precise definitions, and make sincere efforts to understand and apply these definitions.

Please do not assume you understand what these definitions mean simply by reading the words. The meanings behind the definitions reveal themselves only through your own personal daily application of Lean principles and practices. This is a very important point that most people ignore.

The Lean management system is defined as [4]:

"A non-zero-sum principle-based management system focused on creating value for end-use customers and eliminating waste, unevenness, and unreasonableness using the scientific method."

Let's have a close look at the individual parts of this definition. In non-zero-sum activities, all parties share in the gains; the so-called win-win. In contrast, zero-sum activities are when one party gains at the expense of others (win-lose). Zero-sum thinking and actions are much easier to achieve and therefore more common in organizations than non-zero-sum, despite the fact that zero-sum undercuts organizational capability-building, reduces employee involvement (teamwork), and impedes the ability of the organization to respond to changing conditions.

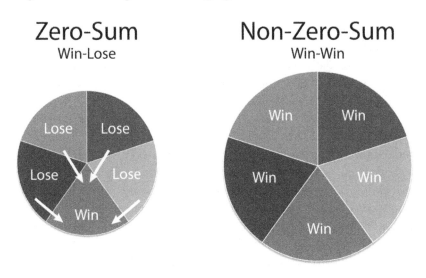

It is important to understand that non-zero-sum outcomes are rarely a perfect win-win. But, they can often be very close or exactly that. Think of it this way: While one or more stakeholders may not win as much as they would like, they do not lose as much as they could. With zero-sum outcomes, one or more stakeholders consistently tend to lose big.

Zero-sum outcomes and decisions are shortcuts, where shortcut is defined as [5]:

> "A more direct route than the customary one,
> or a means of saving time or effort."

Shortcuts, while often very attractive, indicate a mindset where the result matters more than the process. Shortcuts are common in conventional management practice, thus exposing the focus on results. In Lean management, both process and result matter. To get consistently good results requires processes to be understood much better than they normally are. This detailed understanding comes from daily application of the scientific method to problems. I characterize universities as businesses in recognition of the simple fact that they offer products and services that people pay for. However, we all recognize that universities engage in other important activities to fulfill their purpose that may not fit within the scope of traditional business thinking or practice. This should not be a source of conflict because Lean management does not seek to turn all aspects of university work into business-like activities. The fit will be better in some areas than others, but no area is exempt from the need for improvement. The overriding interest is to continuously improve processes in non-zero-sum ways that are beneficial to all key stakeholders – whether they exist in administration, academics, or anywhere else.

The definition of business is [6]:

"Commercial, industrial, or professional dealings."

University is commercial because it engages in commerce (in whole and part), industrial because higher education is an industry (production and sale of services), and professional because dedicated and educated people occupy administrative, faculty, and staff positions and deal with other professionals (current and future).

Notice that business is not formally defined as zero-sum. It is people – managers in particular – who make business zero-sum. In Lean management, we seek to ensure that business is non-zero-sum, because this is the condition that best satisfies people's basic desires. Nobody wants to be the loser.

The word "system" in the above definition of Lean management means:

An organized and consistent set of principles and practices.

In contrast, conventional management is ad hoc and reactionary as conditions dictate.

Despite the appearance of organization and consistency, conventional management suffers greatly from disorganization and inconsistency, as well as logical inconsistencies and false assumptions. For example, the President says, "Having a Ph.D. qualifies you to teach." Yet, possessing a Ph.D. does not assure teaching abilities. This assumption is either naïve or an excuse to avoid all problems that exist in teaching and evade leadership responsibility.

The Lean management system is built on a foundation of two critical principles [7]. Both are required for its correct practice and success:

"Continuous Improvement" and "Respect for People"

The "Continuous Improvement" principle means to improve continuously (daily), not intermittently (e.g. four times per year) or only when forced to improve (e.g. once every 50 years). Therefore, Lean practitioners are always looking for process problems (called "abnormalities") that they can improve. The more one looks, the more one finds abnormalities that can be corrected.

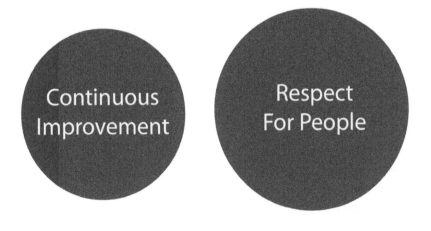

The "Respect for People" principle has been part of progressive management in one form or another almost from the beginning. Why? Because each of the pioneers of progressive management realized that people would not participate in improvement activities if they were not respected (e.g. unemployed as a result of improvement). "People" means stakeholders in the narrow context, but also humanity in the larger context.

You must clearly understand the following: "Respect for People" enables "Continuous Improvement." There is overwhelming empirical evidence that "Continuous Improvement" does not enable "Respect for People." It is common to see application of the "Continuous Improvement" principle disable the "Respect for People" principle in management's drive for short-term cost reduction. In other words, by ignoring the "Respect for People" principle, others are harmed through zero-sum outcomes. This is a fundamental error.

The term "stakeholders" identifies the five key groups of people that have long-term interests in a university's success:

Employees, suppliers, customers,
investors, and communities.

Universities have other important stakeholders such as alumni, foundations, employers, etc. Competitors, which all universities have, can be important stakeholders as well because they often collaborate in research, academic programs, etc.

In Lean management, particular attention is given to "end-use customers" because they are the stakeholder that defines value. Therefore, the "voice of the customer" is a very important point of focus, determined using a process called Quality Function Deployment. Generally, this refers to the person who pays for and uses the service. Sometimes, the person who uses the service is different from the person who pays for the service. In that case, the perception of value must be determined by speaking to both the user and the payer. Various things are done in Lean management to help assure that the value proposition is understood as it changes over time.

The service delivered can narrowly focus on satisfying the end-use customer's perception of value. It can also be a combination of the known features plus other features that the service provider must deliver – i.e. features that the end-use customer wants but cannot clearly articulate, or features that are required by law, policy, or outside party such as an accrediting body.

The idea is to deliver the value proposition that end-use customers desire; to get as close as possible to the actual value proposition. Doing this has the added benefit of reducing costs by eliminating what does not add value. Much can be done to improve the value proposition in higher education without compromising academic rigor. While this should always be a concern, it must never be a reason to avoid making sincere efforts to improve the value proposition on an ongoing basis. Faculty can do many simple, practical, and reasonable things to improve teaching that will greatly improve the value proposition for students and payers, as described in this book.

Most service organizations, including universities, process information using the batch-and-queue method in both academic and administrative work. Batch-and-queue is defined as:

> A method of producing goods or services in which
> large batches of work (information) are processed
> that sit idle in queues for long periods of time
> between processing steps.

The following image depicts this situation.

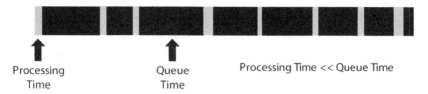

↑
Processing
Time

↑
Queue
Time

Processing Time << Queue Time

This processing method is resource intensive and results in high costs, lengthy delays, quality problems, and frequent re-work. In Lean management, we reduce batch sizes and identify and eliminate queues. Why? Because we are striving to achieve flow, which is less resource intensive and results in lower costs, fewer delays, higher quality, and less re-work. Flow, while difficult to achieve, results in better outcomes for all key stakeholders.

By understanding processes, we begin to see the myriad problems associated with batch-and-queue processing. We begin to see and understand waste, unevenness, and unreasonableness. Waste is defined as [8]:

> "Any activity that consumes resources
> but creates no value for the customer."

The resources consumed can be of any type: time, material, money, facilities, energy, labor, equipment, space, etc. Lean management recognizes eight types of waste [9, 10]:

- Defects
- Transportation
- Overproduction
- Waiting
- Processing
- Movement
- Inventory
- Behaviors

Each of these eight types of waste exist in service businesses, just as they do in any organization. The context for the eighth waste is human behaviors. Meaning, people can behave in ways that add cost but create no value. Alternatively, this can be understood as behaviors that do not add value and can be eliminated [10].

As mentioned previously, Lean management considers students (and payers) as customers. Specifically, they are end-use customers.

This perspective helps provide needed focus and clarity on understanding their interests. Faculty typically determine, in isolation, what is important for students to know. As a result, they often miss opportunities to impart other relevant knowledge.

Referring to students as customers does not mean that faculty relinquish their role in determining what students need to know. Nor does it mean that any silly knowledge or information will be added to courses or programs simply because students ask for it. Nor does it mean students can ignore their responsibilities.

It means that the process for determining what students need to know becomes widened to include other perspectives, and more carefully considered in relation to factors that help shape end-use customers' perceptions of value. Improved academic rigor must be part of efforts to improve value. Customers want that, as do other stakeholders.

In Lean management, the word value means [11]:

"The inherent worth of a product as judged by
the customer and reflected in its selling
price and market demand."

We recognize that people's sense of the value of an individual course or degree program is subjective, but will not let this deter us from making sincere efforts to understand and improve value from end-use customers' perspectives. This definition should not be confused with the word "value" as used in the context of financial terms such as "shareholder value," "enterprise value," "value investing," etc.

While waste is abundant in batch-and-queue processes – often as much as 90 percent of the process – unevenness and unreasonableness are often overlooked. They must not be overlooked. Unevenness is defined as [12]:

Work activities, information, or leadership behaviors that fluctuate significantly.

Unreasonableness is defined as [13]:

Overburdening people or equipment.

Unevenness and unreasonableness are important in Lean management because, like waste, they are also important in improving value and helping to achieve non-zero-sum outcomes. Kaizen is the principal process used to identify and eliminate waste, unevenness, and unreasonableness, and thus to improve processes. The Japanese word "kaizen" means [14]:

"Change for the better."

The context of "change for the better" is multilateral. This is extremely important and something that most people fail to recognize. Without the multilateral context for improvement, kaizen becomes a zero-sum (win-lose) activity. Meaning, the process is improved at someone else's expense. That is not kaizen. For an improvement to qualify as an actual improvement, it must not negatively impact upstream or downstream processes or people. Nor can it negatively impact internal or external stakeholders. Kaizen must be non-zero-sum (win-win); that is a fixed requirement.

With kaizen, you learn to see things as you have never seen them, before. Supra-critical thinking makes you much smarter.

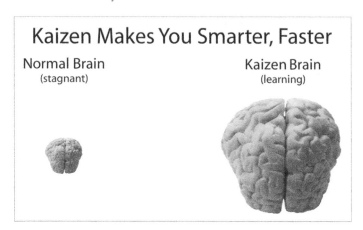

There are three principles for kaizen. They must be followed in order for kaizen to function correctly [14]:

- Process and results
- System focus
- Non-blaming, non-judgmental

Kaizen is used to make small improvements on a daily basis. It can also lead to rapid, big improvements. Kaizen is a preferred approach to improvement because infrequent, large step-function changes are much more difficult for people to achieve. One important result from kaizen is improved information flow. This occurs through large reductions in the number and duration of queues and the number of processing steps.

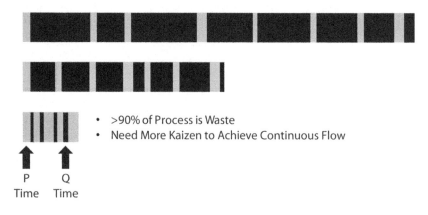

The terms "buyers' markets" and "sellers' markets" helps us understand the position that universities occupy in the marketplace of higher education services available to students and payers. These terms are defined as:

> A buyers' market is a competitive marketplace where many universities (sellers) exist to satisfy customers' (buyers') wants and needs. This type of market typically favors buyers' interests.

> A sellers' market is a non-competitive marketplace where one or two universities (sellers) exist to satisfy customers' (buyers') wants and needs. This type of market typically favors sellers' interests.

University leaders are often ignorant of these market types, or confuse them and remain university-focused when they should be customer-focused. Higher education is not a sellers' market, though for decades it has been managed as if it were – hence, the many problems we see today. Higher education has always been a buyers' market, and will be even more so in the future as it becomes disaggregated and globalized. Students have numerous choices to select from, even among the top-tier universities. Recognizing that students have choices removes a barrier that stands in the way of continuous improvement and of respecting people. Both administrators and faculty will be far better served by listening to the voice of the (student) customer than by ignoring it [15].

While university leaders may like to think their institution has no competition, the fact is that it does. It is essential to accept this fact; failure to do so will usually result in bad outcomes. Recognizing that students have choices removes a barrier that stands in the way of continuous improvement and of respecting people.

Various Lean tools and methods have been developed over the years to help people understand the current process condition and to identify improvement opportunities to achieve a better future state process. The tools have their origins in early 1900s industrial engineering, but were expanded and greatly improved by industrial engineers in post-World War II Japan [16, 17]. Many of the improvements in Lean tools and methods came from industrial engineers at Toyota or its affiliated companies.

These tools and methods have near-universal applicability because their function is simply to help people understand and improve a process – regardless of whether it is a manufacturing or service process. The tools and methods have names that are unfamiliar to most faculty. A few are presented here because they will appear in Chapter 3. A more complete description of Lean tools and methods can be found elsewhere [8, 16].

Lean Management System

A Non-Zero-Sum Principle-Based Management System Focused on Creating Value for End-Use Customers and Eliminating Waste, Unevenness, and Unreasonableness Using the Scientific Method.

Continuous Improvement • Respect for People		Principles
Create Value for Customers — Balance / Harmony		Key Objectives
Stable Long-Term Growth — Innovation		

5S	Kanban	
A3 Reports	Standardized Work	
Just-in-Time*	Jidoka*	
Kaizen	Takt Time	Methods and Tools
Percent Loading Charts	Total Productive Maintenance	
Policy Deployment	Value Stream Maps	
Product-Quantity Analysis	Visual Workplace	
Quality Function Deployment	Work Cells, etc.	

*Toyota Production System principles

The key process improvement tools or methods relevant to improving courses include:

- Five S – An abbreviation for Sort, Straighten, Shine, Standardize, Sustain. Important for establishing an organized workplace and improving quality.

- Just-in-Time – Subsequent process acquires information from the preceding process when needed, in the quantity needed, at the location needed.

- Load smoothing – Called "heijunka" in Japanese. Used to smooth fluctuations in workloads.

- Standardized work – A one-page description of the sequence of work to be performed in a process.

- Visual controls – Signs and other forms of visual information that make it easy to comprehend important information at-a-glance.

Finally, one result of the application of Lean principles and practices is that the benefits must be apparent to students and payers. The improvements must be easily recognized as beneficial to them. Therefore, the following outcomes must occur:

- Students' and payers' perception of value must increase for a constant (or higher) price through improved features and benefits.

or,

- Cost reduction must be passed on to students and payers while improving their perception of value.

There cannot be a situation, for example, where a new technology dramatically lowers the cost of instruction while tuition prices remain flat or increase. Nor can there be a situation where tuition price reduction destroys the value of educational services or of the degree. These are the wrong outcomes for students and payers (and all other stakeholders).

Lean is a top-down management system where buy-in among all members of the senior management team is required. More than simple buy-in, however, top university administrators must apply Lean principles and practices daily to their own work. That means, they must be consistent: words and actions must match. In most cases, words fail to match actions.

While Lean is introduced to organizations top-down, that does not mean it is acceptable to force it onto university personnel. Leaders must lead, and gain buy-in for Lean management by explaining and demonstrating its wide-ranging benefits. However, leaders are often unable to do this because they think Lean is something that other people to do – the people below them in the organization. Lean management is for everyone, not just lower-level employees. Leaders must not confuse knowledge of Lean management (such as reading this book) with having actually practiced Lean management. When it comes to Lean management, there is a saying to keep in mind:

> "Don't confuse getting an A or receiving a
> diploma with knowing anything."

We can also say:

> "Don't confuse being a trustee, president,
> provost, etc., with knowing anything."

Why such strong statements? Because leaders understand batch-and-queue information processing, but they know nothing about flow. Leaders think they treat people with respect, but that is not possible when information is processed batch-and-queue. Hence, the strong statements. You should perceive these statements as representing wonderful new learning opportunities. If you do, then university employees will also.

You are learning something completely new with Lean management. By way of metaphor, you may know how to play the trumpet well (call it batch-and-queue), but you are now asked to play the drums (flow). The two could not be more different, and you must start anew to learn how to play the drums. So, to learn Lean management – to understand and practice it – some humility is required.

You may say, "This is just too much! Who is this idiot telling me I don't know anything?" I am telling you this because I am extremely concerned about the harm to people (e.g. layoffs) caused by senior managers who misunderstand and misapply Lean management. From a historical perspective, there is good reason for me to worry.

If you feel that I have offended you, then there are alternatives to Lean management that you may want to consider. You can do what other university leaders have recently done, such as those at the University of North Carolina [18] and Berkeley [19]: Hire Bain & Company to do a study and inform you of how to achieve "operational excellence" (i.e. cut your budget). For $3,000,000 you will learn from Bain what you could have easily read in *The Chronicle of Higher Education* for $40 (a six month online subscription):

- Reduce layers of management and
- increase span of control.
- Leverage procurement spend.
- Reorganize purchasing, finance, human
- resources, and research office.
- Reduce number of "Centers."
- Consolidate information technology.
- Decrease energy consumption.
- Improve classroom utilization.

- Privatize public assets.

Doing this is a waste of money and does nothing to address problems in academics, which is the locus of the value proposition in higher education. Further, this zero-sum approach, also applied to academics (i.e. cut academic department budgets), marginalizes key stakeholders and results in mostly one-time gains. There will be no creativity or learning among university personnel, no teamwork, and no buy-in.

If you do not like the expensive consultant-led approach to budget cutting, then you can always do-it-yourself. Here is your zero-sum to-do list:

Staff: Furloughs, salary freezes, cut wages and benefits, reduce hours, delay hiring, lay off staff, etc.

Faculty: Furloughs, salary freezes, cut wages and benefits, reduce hours, reduce or eliminate overload pay, delay hiring, layoff faculty, hire more adjuncts (and let faculty manage supply of adjuncts), increase number of students to run grad or undergrad courses, etc.

Academics: Close departments and programs, combine departments and programs, reduce course sections, offer more courses online (pre-recorded, of course), etc.

Students: Reduce scholarships, require students to tutor underclass, reduce teaching assistantships, cut athletic programs, eliminate student clubs, increase class size, cancel classes, cut student services, etc.

Facilities: Delay construction, delay renovations, outsource maintenance, demolish expensive old buildings, lease trucks and heavy equipment, cut contractors, etc.

Administration: Raise prices, have administrators teach courses, reduce or eliminate travel, four-day workweek, differential tuition pricing, outsource IT / HR / legal / bookstore, increase fundraising, spend down the endowment, share services with other campuses or universities, leverage purchases with other campuses or universities, expand administrator duties, cut consultants, cut food in meetings, cut library book and journal budgets, increase room temperature in summer, decrease room temperature in winter, negotiate lower prices for food / electricity / oil / gas / IT service contracts, reduce telecommunications expense, use open source software, improve classroom utilization, put the endowment in higher yield (riskier) investments, etc.

Do these in any combination and repeat as necessary. There is no skill in doing that, and more harm than good will come of it.

These actions occur because of long-term neglect, perhaps caused by leaders thinking the university perpetually enjoys a sellers' market. Whatever the case, you should be very careful because this zero-sum, non-human-centered approach to problem-solving will create even greater amounts of waste, unevenness, and unreasonableness.

Remarkably, this cut-my-way to improvement method is characterized in the business and higher education press as "creative solutions." There is nothing creative about it. These pedestrian zero-sum actions will marginalize key stakeholders and yield mostly one-time gains. There will be no creativity or learning among university personnel, little teamwork, and almost no buy-in. And, nothing has been done to address the problems in academic programs and courses.

Remember what I said. When it comes to Lean management:

> "Don't confuse being a trustee, president,
> provost, etc., with knowing anything."

That is also because university administrators and others (including expensive consultants) consistently and incorrectly view cost problems narrowly as budget problems, when instead cost problems are actually process problems. Costs are subordinate to processes, and everyone needs a lot of help to see that. Lean helps you see that. You can see that only if you are willing to learn new things. Adopting Lean management will be a lot of work, and the benefits will not come easy. Do not even think about taking shortcuts.

You have a choice: Do what everyone else does – cut, cut, cut – and never actually address what ails your university. Be prepared, then, for recurring problems where the only solution you know is more cuts. People will be upset, frustrated, and more committed to their own well-being than to the university.

Or, you can do something that directly addresses your problems in ways that energize and engage people. Rise to a challenge befitting university leaders: Adopt Lean management in academic (as well as in administrative [20] processes) and learn how to practice it correctly [21]. Conflict is not free; try making people happy instead.

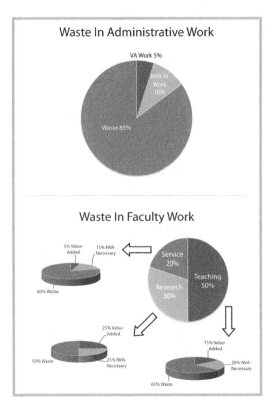

Notes

[1] F.W. Taylor, *Scientific Management: Comprising Shop Management, Principles of Scientific Management, Testimony Before the House Committee*, Foreword by Harlow S. Person, Harper & Brothers Publishers, New York, NY, 1947, p. 191. Note: People strongly associate Taylor's work with manufacturing. But that is not how Taylor thought of his work. In the Introduction to *The Principles of Scientific Management*, Taylor said (p. 8): "The illustrations chosen... will especially to engineers and to managers of industrial and manufacturing establishments... It is hoped, however, that it will be clear to other readers that the same principles can be applied with equal force to all social activities: to the management of our homes; the management of our farms... of our churches, our philanthropic institutions, our universities, and our governmental departments." Ignoring Taylor's work because of incorrect perceptions results in close-mindedness that can harm organizations and impair their ability to fulfill their purpose.

[2] These common mistakes are indicative of two major and widespread teaching failures in higher education: conducting research and critical thinking. It seems that most students graduate thinking that assignments requiring research were senseless academic exercises that are not useful in the real world. Once in the workforce, they misunderstand and misapply ideas, concepts, and practices, which then cause harm to others. Doing research could have helped avoid doing harm. Second, the level of critical thinking that professors teach to students is inadequate for the challenges that many of them will face as managers, whose work will have a huge impact on other people's lives and livelihoods. I use the article "For Lean Factories, No Buffer" *The Wall Street Journal* (T. Aeppel, 29 April 2011) as an example of how a systematic failure to do research by the CEO, a purchasing executive, consultants, and an economist results in bad outcomes. Many such articles can be plucked from the real world and used in class to illustrate the importance of research and supra-critical thinking post-graduation.

[3] Y. Monden, *Toyota Management System: Linking the Seven Key Functional Areas*, Productivity Press, Portland, OR, 1997

[4] B. Emiliani, *Practical Lean Leadership: A Strategic Leadership Guide for Executives*, The CLBM, LLC, Wethersfield, Conn., 2008, p. 10

[5] *The American Heritage College Dictionary*, 3rd edition, Houghton Mifflin Co., New York, 1997, p. 1261

[6] *The American Heritage College Dictionary*, 3rd edition, Houghton Mifflin Co., 1997, p. 190

[7] "The Toyota Way 2001," Toyota Motor Corporation, internal document, Toyota City, Japan, April 2001

[8] *Lean Lexicon*, 4th edition, Lean Enterprise Institute, Cambridge, MA, September 2008, p. 112

[9] T. Ohno, *Toyota Production System*, Productivity Press, Portland, OR, 1988, pp. 19-20

[10] M.L. Emiliani, "Lean Behaviors," *Management Decision*, Vol. 36, No. 9, 1998, pp. 615-631

[11] *Lean Lexicon*, 4th edition, Lean Enterprise Institute, Cambridge, MA, September 2008, p. 109

[12] Note 4, p. 13

[13] Note 4, p. 13

[14] M. Imai, "Basics of Kaizen I," Kaizen Institute of America seminar at The Hartford Graduate Center, Hartford, Conn., March 1990, p. II-3

[15] A strong argument against referring to students as customers was made by a professor in response to a recent article that appeared in *The Chronicle of Higher Education*. The professor said that in a normal transaction, the supplier has a large burden of activity, while the customer has a small burden of activity. For example, a restaurant (supplier) has a lot of work to do to fulfill a customer's dinner order, while the customer has only a little work to do. In higher education, the opposite is true. The student has a lot of work to do, while the professor (supplier) has a little work to do (sum of preparation, class time, and grading time per week). However, this assumes learning *must* be difficult and it *must* be time-consuming. To what extent do professors make it that way? Why do they do that?

[16] J. Liker, *The Toyota Way*, McGraw-Hill, New York, NY, 2004

[17] J. Shook, *Managing to Learn: Using the A3 Management Process*, Lean Enterprise Institute, Cambridge, MA, 2008

[18] "The University of North Carolina at Chapel Hill, Cost Diagnostic: Final Report Summary," Bain & Company, Boston, MA, July 2009, http://universityrelations.unc.edu/budget/documents/2009/Bain%20Report%20Summary%20%20Notes.pdf

[19] "Achieving Operational Excellence at University of California, Berkeley, Final Diagnostic Report, Complete Version," Bain & Company, Boston, MA, April, 2010, http://oe.berkeley.edu/sites/default/files/diagnostic%20report%20bain%20uc%20berkeley.pdf

[20] W. Balzer, *Lean Higher Education: Increasing the Value and Performance of University Processes*, CRC Press, Boca Raton, Fla., 2010

[21] B. Emiliani, *Moving Forward Faster: The Mental Evolution from Fake Lean to REAL Lean*, The CLBM, LLC, Wethersfield, Conn., 2011

2

Brief History of Continuous Improvement in Higher Education

In the early 1900s, business leaders in America were critical of higher education and the graduates coming out of its colleges and universities. There were concerns about the cost of university education and the quality of the output. One university leader received many complaints such as [1]: "That cub [graduate] you sent down here thinks this is a university. He won't work."

Frederick Taylor was also critical of college and university education, and had this to say about engineering graduates [2]:

"...failure to recognize the importance of
punctuality and the value of time and discipline."

"...inability to concentrate on an undertaking and
bring it through to a conclusion."

"...they cannot get away from this habit
of absorbing..."

"...lack of appreciation of the point of view
of the workingman."

Taylor generally viewed engineering graduates as lazy and undisciplined; disdainful of routine activities; absorbers of information while producing little; lacking hands-on work experience; and behaving in condescending ways to workers. The latter two were of particular concern to Taylor because about half of all graduates would go on to become managers but they did not know the workers that they managed.

Taylor, a tennis athlete, felt that intramural athletics was highly beneficial to student's education. He said [3]: "...I should look upon foot-ball [sic] and the training received in athletics as one of the most useful elements in a college course, for two reasons: First, because in it they are actuated by a truly serious purpose; and second, because they are there given, not the elective idea of doing what they want to do, but cooperation, and cooperation of the same general character which they will be called upon to practice in after [university] life."

Taylor felt that the competitive experience of intramural athletics and the need for cooperation on a team served the future workers and managers of industry well. It would help graduates develop close personal contact with the workingman and managers.

Criticisms such as these led to a study by Morris Cooke and funded by The Carnegie Foundation for the Advancement of Teaching. Cooke, a mechanical engineer, was a close associate of Frederick Winslow Taylor. He was selected to do the study based on his extensive experience improving industrial organizations using Taylor's system of Scientific Management [4]. Cooke's background provided a comparative basis for observing and evaluating academic institutions, from which recommendations for improvement were made.

Cooke wrote a report titled "Academic and Industrial Efficiency" in 1910 [5]. In it, he explained his charge was to (p. 3): "...obtain an estimate of the cost and of the output both in teaching and in research in the departments of physics..." of eight colleges and universities visited (seven in U.S.A., one in Canada).

The preface was written by Henry S. Pritchett, a past president of Massachusetts Institute of Technology and president of The Carnegie Foundation for the Advancement of Teaching at the time Cooke's work was commissioned and completed. In the Preface of the report, Pritchett said (p. v): "The cost of university education has risen throughout the world, but nowhere so rapidly as in the United States." He also said (p. vi): "The college is partly a business and partly something very different from a business. Mr. Cooke is concerned only with the former aspect."

Pritchett viewed the administration of a university as resembling a business, that teaching does not resemble a business but should, and that research does not resemble a business and cannot – to which he said (p. iii): "…the industrial point of view is obviously inapplicable." That means Cooke's focus would be on administration and teaching – the business parts of higher education, and less on research.

Interestingly, today's view is not the same as Pritchett's view. Administration of a university is increasingly seen as a business that can benefit from systems, methods, and tools developed by industry (though the systems, methods, and tools are often misunderstood and improperly applied). Teaching still does not resemble a business, but it should. And research has become huge business – though not very "efficient," as Cooke would say.

Cooke was quick to note that every university thinks it is different (p.5): "…every college feels like it has problems unalike, and of greater difficulty of solution than, those to be encountered at other colleges." Yet, the problems universities face are easier compared to other businesses (p. 5): "…uniformity in collegiate management is a much easier problem than it is in most industries, because… the individual plants vary considerably more than do the colleges."

Cooke commented on how university administrators and faculty members think what they do is unique, and that there is little to be learned from others outside of academia (p. 6): "It is impossible to avoid the conclusion… that the men connected with colleges and universities have looked upon their functions as having very little in common with those which engage the attention of people in other walks of life; and any one making such a study as this is first of all impressed with the price that is being paid to maintain this position of isolation."

He identified the ills of university administration and academic units as bureaucratic and requiring many reviews and approvals; large amounts of time spent discussing nonsense issues and thus making no progress (called "log rolling" in those days); no gauge of efficiency; administration has responsibility but no authority;

academic departments have too much autonomy; a lack of cooperation between departments; poorly executed committee management; and that faculty routinely do work that should be done by lower paid people.

With respect to teaching, Cooke said (p. 19): "One is struck in any such study of collegiate conditions with the absence of any gauge of efficiency..." He goes on to say (p. 19): "...before any progress is possible [to measure performance and compare work between departments and institutions] some selection [metric] must be made [established], and the writer wishes to suggest as perhaps the most immediately available unit the student-hour. By a student-hour is meant one hour of lectures, of laboratory work, or recitation work, for a single pupil. Thus, a section of thirty students on a three hours' laboratory period would mean ninety student-hours... With this as a basis, we can get some tally of the efficiency with which the buildings are operated, the cost of undergraduate teaching, and each of several other items which go to make up the expenses of a university." This is where the credit-hour originated.

In trying to make sense of academic work, Cooke drew analogies to what he was familiar with, industrial concerns, and saw the college teacher as the producer – one whose labor results in something that is produced – and that they could learn useful things from others to improve their own work (p. 21): "...important changes come from within... it will be a gain if professors will more willingly seek to profit by suggestions derived from the world outside... The college professor must take the position that he is not an individual set apart..." In other words, the work that faculty do in teaching is, in its fundamentals, more similar than different to the work that others do. The role of the teacher is that of a "producer" of teaching.

Importantly, Cooke saw that teaching efficiency could be improved, but that it must be done in non-zero-sum (win-win) way (p. 21): "...an increase in their efficiency... will result in larger work accomplished and hence in larger remuneration without relatively larger cost to the institutions." Teachers who teach more should receive higher pay for the additional work. This follows from a key element of the Scientific Management system, where higher output must result in higher pay for workers. (See Notes 6 and 7 for wonderful descriptions of meaning and intent of Taylor's Scientific Management).

Cooke also felt that teachers' time should be spent teaching and with students, and not doing administrative work (p. 22-23): "Everything must be done to safeguard the time of the teacher.... taking inventories, keeping track of appropriations, mimeographing examination papers...These things are clerical work, and should be handled outside of the teaching field, and not as part of the teacher's duties." Today, university teachers spend much of their time doing just such activities.

Cooke looked at the time teachers spend with students and felt it should be increased by transferring administrative duties to others (p. 24): "...[professors] probably spend less than three hours a day with students. This is the equivalent of what is generally called the 'productive' time of other workers." He also noted that the long hours that teachers work would never be permitted in other businesses (p. 27-28): "Another point which operates against efficiency of the teaching staff is their long hours... The college professor probably gets less help out of recreation... than almost any other class of worker... it is impossible to believe that men with so little relaxation do not suffer from this excessive concentration... It is hardly possible that such hours would be permitted in an industrial establishment."

In addition to criticizing the number of hours worked, Cooke also criticized teacher's participation on committee work (p. 28): "...[there is] comparatively little time spent on committee work; but as a source of interruption to the regular work of a teacher, committee meetings are undoubtedly a great, and in a large measure unnecessary annoyance." He felt that committee work should be handled by administrators, as was the case in industry, and let the "producers" produce.

With respect to research, Cooke noted the emerging trend of Federally sponsored research and of faculty being pulled in different directions (p. 30): "The fact that apparently there is to be a great increase in the energy with which research is to be pursued at colleges makes research a vital matter in a study of the efficiency with which it is conducted... the physics teachers I met are included in one of these two classes: first, those who would like to... give their efforts to developing the teaching side, and second, those who feel that their teaching hours are so much time taken away from research... One man high in the councils of his department told me that his abilities lay in the direction of teaching, and that the efforts that were being made to drive him into research work were against efficiency."

He went on to say (p. 31): "...to-day a man can become an acknowledged efficient teacher without adding materially to his professional reputation or his earning value. To accomplish the latter he must... do research work and publish the results of it." Thus, Cooke expressed his concern about how the emerging need to make a name for one's self by doing research would result in a loss of focus on teaching. Indeed.

Finally, Cooke noted how faculty's interest in teaching was greater for students majoring in physics and less for those who took a physics course to satisfy a program requirement (p. 34): "...the individual student who gives promise of becoming a research worker, or who is going into physics as a life work, received the lion's share of attention. At some places the large undergraduate classes of students who were studying physics simply as a culture study [gen ed requirement] were looked upon as the least important part of the work of the department."

These observations and findings ring true today, over 100 years later. In general, it seems that much remains the same. For example:

- Each university thinks it is unique or different in important ways. This means that systems, methods, and tools used for improvement will not immediately be seen as transferrable from one institution to another.

- Faculty remain inward-looking and resistant to ideas from outside academia (especially business, and fail to distinguish the good from the bad. It is not all bad). They continue to pay a price for this.

- Faculty remain engaged in clerical and related activities that consume time that would be better spent doing other things. This could help reduce long hours (evening and weekend work).

- Committee work is part of shared governance, something which Cooke did not seem to understand, much as others do not understand today. Nevertheless, faculty might consider which elements of shared governance are most important to participate in and leave the rest to administration.

- The ills of administration and academic units remain largely the same.

- Pressure to do research and establish one's reputation have escalated significantly. While research can be highly complementary to teaching, it can also cause teaching to suffer – in part because it is often allowed by administrators to be a lower priority.

Morris Cooke's report was controversial in its day. The faculty who read it generally did not like it and did not agree with Cooke's observations or findings. A record of the push-back can be found in the Proceedings of the Conference on Scientific Management held on 12-14 October 1911 at The Amos Tuck School of Administration and Finance at Dartmouth College in Hanover, New Hampshire [8]. In a session titled "Round Table Discussions:

The Application of Scientific Management in Certain Industries" [9], the faculty present supported the view that Scientific Management was applicable to administrative activities but pushed back hard on its applicability to teaching and research. To them, teaching was different in every way to the work performed by factory laborers with whom they associated Scientific Management. The faculty felt that business people's view of higher education was flawed, and that its purpose differs from and lies above business: to serve society vs. serving shareholders. Therefore, higher education was not subject to the same rules or practices as business.

Professor Edwin Bartlett of Dartmouth College said (p. 289): "It is not to be admitted that education should be business-like except in the case of being well organized and without waste…" They felt the cost driver was administration, not instruction, that teaching and research are creative activities that could not be standardized, and that only peers can judge competency of faculty – not markets.

What seems apparent from the discussion was that the learned did not want to learn. Faculty focused on the reasons why Scientific Management would not work in the academic part of colleges and universities. It represents a failure among the faculty to think and investigate, and satisfaction with immense variation in teaching and the status quo – despite Frank Gilbreth's passionate pleas for gaining a common understanding and implementing Cooke's recommendations for improvement.

Agreement was reached on the following six points:

- Standardized syllabi and lecture notes could be used, especially first and second year courses.

- There should be a division of labor so that faculty can focus on teaching and research. Transfer "trivial activities… to cheaper men."

- Faculty can be cross-trained to teach different courses.

- Senior faculty should coach junior faculty.

- The university should hire more tutors to avoid "spoiled work" (drop-outs).

- Adopt the student-hour metric.

It seems that the biggest thing to come out of Cooke's report was the student-hour metric. Other points of agreement exist, but vary from institution to institution or department to department. In summary, Cooke's work was largely ignored.

Then, as now, faculty needed to learn about improvement via other means as well as their own because teaching is a driver of student satisfaction. Nobody is immune from the need to improve, in part because universities compete. It is a buyers' market for higher education services.

After Cooke's work, there is evidence in the literature of many efforts by faculty, usually singly or in pairs, to improve their own courses and their degree programs. Much of the activity has taken place post-1970, and uses specific improvement methods such as assessment (feedback) instruments, total quality management, (TQM), quality function deployment (QFD), hoshin kanri (strategy deployment), etc.

The QFD and hoshin kanri papers referenced in Notes 11, 12 should be studied because these processes help assure the value proposition is actually improved (QFD) and that an organization's efforts are properly focused on the right improvement activities (hoshin kanri) in preference to random improvement.

TQM seems to have been the only approach to improvement applied university-wide, mainly in the 1980s and 1990s. It nearly always ended in failure because TQM lacked the means by which to realize institutional goals. The "what" was easy to define, but the "how" (how to do it) was lacking. Generally, it has left university employees with strong negative feelings about large-scale improvement and anything that comes from industry. These negative perceptions must be overcome for Lean management to succeed.

Beginning in the mid-1990s, more people in service businesses began to realize that the management system used by progressive manufacturers – which yielded spectacular gains in productivity, cost reduction, and quality improvement – could be used in service businesses as well. They finally abandoned their position of isolation and became receptive to suggestions from a world outside their own.

Unfortunately, most senior managers cherry-picked the parts they thought they needed and ignored the rest. As a result, the integrity of the management system was compromised and results fell far short of expectations. Lesson learned: There are right and wrong ways to practice Lean management. It has taken a long time for leaders of service organizations to recognize that Lean management must be used in its entirety.

Having had significant hands-on experience with Lean management prior to entering academia in 1999, I used Lean management as my approach to improvement. I applied Lean principles and practices to the courses that I taught from the very start of my academic career at Rensselaer Polytechnic Institute (Hartford, Conn., campus). This groundbreaking work is described in a paper I wrote in 2004 titled: "Improving Business School Courses by Applying lean Principles and Practices" [10]. It continues to be the approach I use to design and deliver my courses.

In 2002 and 2003 I led the first-ever series of kaizens to improve an accredited graduate degree program. This seminal work is described in a paper I wrote in 2005 titled [11]: "Using Kaizen to Improve Graduate Business School Degree Programs." I also created a manual to help guide and facilitate kaizen, titled: "Team Leader's Kaizen Manual For Academic Courses and Programs" [12].

These two papers describe processes that can be applied to both undergraduate and graduate curricula, and in any school in the university from engineering to business to nursing to arts and sciences.

The significance of this work is that it is specific, practical, and actionable. It provides both the "what" and the "how" for improving the value proposition for individual courses and degree programs. It provides a pathway for faculty to improve their teaching individually. It also provides a pathway for faculty to improve their teaching in teams comprised of key stakeholders: administrators, staff, faculty, alumni, business leaders, and so on.

They do not address the modes of delivery of instruction by teachers. Those who do not speak clearly, are lethargic, or otherwise lacking in in live classroom skills are a problem that should be addressed by different means, some of which will be discussed in subsequent chapters. The main point, however, is to ensure that all of the means used are consistent with the "Respect for People" principle.

My experience with Lean management in industry and academia, as well as my 15 years of research on Lean leadership will serve as the basis for the remaining chapters of this book. It will inform readers of the details of how Lean management should be applied in higher education, both academics and administration [13], to realize favorable outcomes for all key stakeholders.

Notes

[1] B.B. Brackett, "Academic Efficiency," *Science*, Vol. 33, No. 849, 7 April 1911, pp. 528-529

[2] F.W. Taylor "Why Manufacturers Dislike College Graduates," *The Sibley Journal of Engineering*, Vol. 24, February 1910, pp. 196-204 and C.B. Thompson, *The Theory and Practice of Scientific Management*, Houghton Mifflin Company, 1917, p. 194, note 2

[3] "The Dedication of the Engineering Building of the University of Pennsylvania. A Comparison of University and Industrial Discipline and Methods," *Science*, Vol. XXIV, No. 619, 9 November 1906, p. 577-583

[4] F.W. Taylor, *The Principles of Scientific Management*, Harper & Brothers Publishers, New York, NY, 1911. NOTE: People strongly associate Taylor's work with manufacturing. But that is not how Taylor thought of his work. In the Introduction to *The Principles of Scientific Management*, Taylor said (p. 8): "The illustrations chosen... will especially to engineers and to managers of industrial and manufacturing establishments... It is hoped, however, that it will be clear to other readers that the same principles can be applied with equal force to all social activities: to the management of our homes; the management of our farms... of our churches, our philanthropic institutions, our universities, and our governmental departments." Ignoring Taylor's work because of incorrect perceptions results in close-mindedness that can harm organizations and impair their ability to fulfill their purpose.

[5] M.L. Cooke, "Academic and Industrial Efficiency," The Carnegie Foundation for the Advancement of Teaching, Bulletin No. 5, 1910

[6] See Taylor's testimony to Congress in 1912 in F.W. Taylor, *Scientific Management: Comprising Shop Management, Principles of Scientific Management, Testimony Before the House Committee*, Foreword by Harlow S. Person, Harper & Brothers Publishers, New York, NY, 1947

[7] M.L. Cooke, "The Spirit and Social Significance of Scientific Management," *The Journal of Political Economy*, Vol. XXI, No. 6, June 1913, p. 481-493

[8] Dartmouth College Conferences, First Tuck School Conference, Scientific Management: *Addresses and Discussions at the*

Conference on Scientific Management Held October 12, 13, 14, Nineteen Hundred and Eleven, The Amos Tuck School of Administration and Finance, Dartmouth College in Hanover, New Hampshire, The Plimpton Press, Norwood, Massachusetts, 1912

[9] Ibid, pages 286-309, 358, 375.

[10] M.L. Emiliani, "Improving Business School Courses by Applying Lean Principles and Practices," *Quality Assurance in Education*, Vol. 12, No. 4, 2004, pp. 175-187

[11] M.L. Emiliani, "Using Kaizen to Improve Graduate Business School Degree Programs," *Quality Assurance in Education*, Vol. 13, No. 1, 2005, pp. 37-52

[12] M.L. Emiliani, "Team Leader's Kaizen Manual For Academic Courses and Programs," unpublished work, 2002 (updated 2009, 2012, and 2013).

[13] W. Balzer, *Lean Higher Education: Increasing the Value and Performance of University Processes*, CRC Press, Boca Raton, Fla., 2010

3

How Leadership Changes

Lean leadership differs tremendously compared to conventional leadership. This chapter presents many of the ways in which Lean leadership is different, but not all the ways in which it is different. If you embark on the so-called Lean journey, you will learn the truth of what I say here. You will learn even more through your own daily application of Lean principles and practices.

Let's begin with a general comparison between Lean and conventional leadership. Here are some characteristics of conventional leaders:

- Focus is on personal traits (such as charisma), behaviors, and competencies.
- Guard information (sits in queues).
- Process information batch-and-queue.
- Delegate improvement.
- Done learning.
- Principles unclear.
- Results-focused.
- Short-term thinking and actions.
- Zero-sum (win-lose).
- Slow to change.

In contrast, here are some characteristics of Lean leaders:

- Focus is on beliefs, behaviors, and competencies.
- Share information.
- Process information via flow.
- Participate in improvement.
- Never done learning.

- Principles clear: "Continuous Improvement" and Respect for People."
- Process and results focus.
- Long-term; don't sacrifice for short-term gains.
- Non-zero-sum (win-win).
- Change daily.

Importantly, Lean leaders see that part of their role is to get information to flow. They are therefore very sensitive to time. They want to understand processes to find out how long it actually takes to get things done as the number and duration of queues in a process shrink. For example, it takes 9 months to prepare a university budget, but careful analysis of the budgeting process would reveal that 90 percent of the process is waste (information sitting in queue), and contains considerable unevenness and unreasonableness. The actual time people spend working on the budget is one month or less.

Lean people would re-design the process so that university budgets could be prepared in one month, and then set goals to continuous improve the process (reduce the time) it takes to prepare the budget. In doing this, the budget prepared would be more accurate. Recognizing that nobody can predict the future, the budgeting process would continue to be improved and be less of a burden for budget participants to prepare. This would allow them to build budgets more frequently that have greater accuracy and less unfavorable variances that people have to report on, and which typically result in blame.

Likewise in academics, the time it takes to develop a degree program, make a program change, introduce a new course, revise a course, etc., is much longer in duration than the actual time it takes to do the work. Because departments meet monthly, the work sits in queue most of the time. The work submitted to the curriculum committee could sit in queue for up to 719.8 of the 720 hours in that month. Once approved by the curriculum committee, the work once again sits in queue until the change implemented.

While the process many not be difficult, it is lengthy and burdensome on the people who participate in the process. When work is a burden, people will tend to do lower quality work or otherwise be less engaged. It also means that changes to degree programs and courses occur at a rate that is a small fraction of the rate of change in the real world. This is how curricula becomes aged and fails to meet the needs of students and employers. This does not mean that curricula should be changed solely to meet these needs, but they are important needs that educators must dutifully consider.

The glacial pace of work means that higher education will always lag significantly behind the "real world." Higher education would be subject to less criticism from a curriculum standpoint if its processes were more closely in step with the world outside. This is not to say that curricula should be in lock-step with the world outside. Rather, it should be in closer step, given the need for skilled curriculum development and appropriate deliberation to assure high quality educational services.

While people need to rest, information does not need to rest by sitting in queues. If humans need 8 hours of rest per day, information can surely get along with far less rest. A curriculum change does not need to rest for 719.8 hours.

To improve information flow, Lean people would want the curriculum committee to meet weekly for 20 minutes instead of one monthly face-to-face meeting for 2 hours. More frequent meetings and fewer agenda items will result in curriculum changes that are processed more quickly. The meeting schedule could be once per week for 20 minutes via webcam for routine items, and once a month face-to-face for up to 60 minutes. The monthly face-to-face meetings could be for more complex agenda items requiring greater discussion. Lean people, recognizing that problems are good, will work together to make adjustments as necessary to improve this new process.

The same thinking can be applied to department meetings, where individual agenda items are cycled through on a weekly basis. The outcome will be better information flow and more effective use of faculty's time.

These two examples reveal great insensitivity to time and unawareness of flow among university leaders. There is total satisfaction with batch-and-queue information processing, which is always higher cost than flow (financial and otherwise). There are other problems as well, such as incorrect priorities (internal focus vs. student focus, overburdening people with too many things to do, etc.), poor allocation of resources, and so on. The Lean management system is designed to correct these problems commonly found in organizations. But that will happen only if university leaders recognize the many ways they must change – in this case, abandoning batch-and-queue information processing and learning how to achieve flow.

In Lean, managers do not add value; only the producers add value. That is why leaders must serve others, especially the producers. The fact that leaders do not add value means, fundamentally, that their roles and responsibilities will be different than they are in conventional management. Some roles and responsibilities will be exactly the same, some will differ in small but very important ways, others will differ in large ways.

Serving others means knowing what they do in current terms, not past terms (as in, you did that type of work years ago but things are different now). It also means you must become a facilitator rather than one who directs others. For example, if you adopt Lean, most people in your university will have the same reaction to progressive management as employees in manufacturing businesses had over 100 years ago. Employees will complain quietly and loudly, and be very concerned that Lean will be bad for them in the following ways:

- De-humanize them.
- Speed them up and burn them out.

- De-skill them.
- Take away their knowledge.
- Take away their creativity.
- Cost them their job.

From the employees' perspective, progressive management is a major cause for concern. Lean is seen by them as mean. In conventional management, university leaders would not even hear these concerns. The president would simply tell people: "This plan is our new direction. We will move ahead." Obviously, buy-in will be lacking and the pace of change will therefore be very slow. Lean leaders, on the other hand, would recognize that employees have legitimate concerns that must be addressed. If not, information will not flow; it will remain batch-and-queue.

These six concerns clearly inform us of what employees consider very important aspects of not only their jobs, but of their lives. They care about the work they do and how change will affect them personally. They are also concerned that the university may gain at their expense. University employees will be concerned about zero-sum outcomes, whether they have tenure or not. Employees' concerns are fully justified because so many leaders in modern history have ignored the "Respect for People" principle and thus continue practicing zero-sum management. They end up doing harm instead of good.

The six concerns are well-known and consistent over time. Therefore, university leaders must be prepared to answer employees' questions; these are their most basic concerns and simply cannot go unaddressed. Lean leaders will focus time and effort to address employees concerns and thereby reduce and eliminate criticism. University leaders will do this not just through oral arguments, but through personal participation in improvement activities such as kaizen.

When employees see their leaders participating in kaizen, they begin to get the sense that managers are serious about improvement. If all that employees hear from leaders are oral arguments supporting Lean (e.g. "I fully support Lean"), then they will soon conclude it is all talk and something that they can ignore. They should indeed ignore such leaders because they are not leading; they are just talking.

Thus far, we have seen how leadership changes in three important ways. It develops time consciousness and facilitates flow. It engages people, often one-on-one, to help answer their important questions about Lean. And, finally, leaders start to walk the talk by participating in kaizen often (which you will find to be a fun, learning-rich activity – more on that later).

I noted earlier that Lean leaders have a strong process focus [1]. There are practical reasons for this: Good processes yield consistently good result, while bad processes yield consistently bad results. To get good results, the scientific methods must be applied to understand process problems. Thus, the university president with a Ph.D. in literature will have something new to learn to be an effective Lean leader. The university president with a Ph.D. in science or engineering will also have to learn how the scientific method is applied to process improvement.

When processes are bad and yield consistently bad results, there is a strong desire by leaders to blame people overtly or covertly. Blame is not good for one's career, is a huge distraction, and destroys (or stagnates) value. Blame is a shortcut to problem-solving that solves nothing. It reflects the zero-sum mindset of the leader and indifference to the actual cause of the problem. Leaders' lack of curiosity about what went wrong, which is almost always a process problem, soon leads to organizational dysfunction and further batch-and-queue information processing. It is simple to understand: People who fear being blamed for problems keep quiet. Information they possess that other people need to know sits in queue, often for years or decades.

Let's review: Leaders who are results-focused tolerate processes that operate poorly and cause a lot of problems, which leads to blaming people. They are being disrespectful to people in several ways and gain no insight into the actual root causes of problems. Overt and covert blame by leaders is destructive to people and organizations. So, how do you move away from that?

When processes are good and yield consistently good results, then the strong desire to blame people for errors greatly diminishes. When this happens, people can focus more clearly on further improving processes. This is why the "Respect for People" principle is not optional in Lean management. Leaders must practice this principle to enable daily continuous improvement throughout the university. This is what motivates people to experiment and try new things. The pioneers of Lean management learned this by trial-and-error. We are smarter now because of them. You do not have to learn by trial-and-error as they did.

University leaders who adopt Lean will ask their employees to engage in problem-solving activities using new processes and tools. The worst thing that leaders can do is ask employees to do something that they are not willing to do themselves. Leaders will have to use the same processes and tools for the kinds of management problems that they encounter to avoid an instant loss of credibility.

More than that, you will need to show evidence of your use of problem-solving processes and tools to employees. They will need to see examples to know you mean what you say. You should not view this as a burden. Learning these new skills will make you better able to facilitate, evaluate, and improve others' problem-solving work. You will also broadcast the message to followers that you are not done learning, and you will set a good example for others to follow. It also will help you identify future leaders; people who are good at quickly recognizing and correcting problems – and avoiding problems from the start.

For example, administrators say the words "root cause" in reference to the source of the problem, yet they have done no actual root cause analysis. They have not put pen to paper and worked it out using the 5 Whys or fishbone diagram root cause analysis methods. That is no good. You have to work it out for yourself first. Do not delegate it to others. It will be a challenge, but you will learn and improve with practice. In doing your own root cause analyses, you will realize that guessing at the causes of problems only prolongs them. You will also recognize the foolishness of assigning one cause to an effect (a problem), when the problem is in fact the result of numerous causes.

We have now seen how leadership changes in three additional ways. Leadership begins to think in terms of processes. They stop the habit of blaming people for errors. And, they use the same problem-solving processes and tools for the management problems that leaders face.

Next, let's talk about leadership behaviors that are required to be a successful Lean leader. Most conceptualizations of leadership center on leaders' behaviors and personal traits. While important on some levels, Lean leaders are driven by a different belief system that is created by participating in process improvement activities.

In the conventional model, leaders' behaviors result in certain competencies. Change the behavior and you get different competencies [2]. The assumption is that people's beliefs with respect to management are uniform. While perhaps simplifying leadership development models, that is a terrible assumption to make. In Lean, participating in process improvement activities is, for most people, an enormous revelation. Work that they thought took hours, days, or months can be done in minutes. The cost is lower, the quality is higher, the lead-time is shorter, work is smoothed out over time (vs. peaks and valleys), burdens are reduced or eliminated, and so on. Jobs become easier. People like positive outcomes and want more of them to make their job easier in the future. This is what happens when process improvement is done correctly.

It is common to hear people, who participated for years in batch-and-queue processes, exclaim after a day or two of kaizen, "I didn't think it was possible. I would not have believed it if I did not see it with my own eyes!" The experience is a life-changing event. This begins the process of replacing beliefs rooted in batch-and-queue processing with beliefs that are rooted in flow. However, leaders must participate in kaizen to experience such a revelation.

It is common to find leaders who talk about the importance of Lean yet never participate in process improvement, while employees at lower levels are required to. This creates a huge belief (and learning) gap between leaders who remain stuck in the status quo, and employees who are seeing and experiencing dramatically new things. The gap is not sustainable. Leaders leading in their conventional ways will subvert the work of employees trying to achieve flow. Soon, Lean will die, and critics both inside and out will say: "I told you it would not work in higher ed. We're different. Lean is a manufacturing thing."

The differences in beliefs between conventional (batch-and-queue) leaders and employees learning about Lean (flow) drives leaders and followers apart. This is an unavoidable outcome when leaders remain arrogant and think they have nothing new to learn, or who feel uncomfortable participating as regular members on kaizen teams. I can assure you that leaders will be uncomfortable at first. But, so what? Leaders profess to care most about students and the university. If that is true, they can briefly suffer some minor personal discomfort.

It turns out that beliefs inform behaviors, which in turn, result in competencies. Therefore, it is wrong to view new leadership behaviors as the wellspring of new competencies. One has to go deeper into beliefs. It is insufficient to gain new beliefs by reading about them or hearing about them. One must undergo new experiences.

Here are just a few examples of the differences in beliefs, behaviors, and competencies between conventional (batch-and-queue) leaders and Lean (flow) leaders [2, 3]. They are presented in the following format: belief; behavior; competency.

Conventional: Many processing steps are needed; don't question the process; maintain the status quo (and add more steps as needed). **Lean**: Can do the work with fewer steps; question the process; challenge the status quo and improve.

Conventional: Completed unit of work must wait until all work is done to move to the next step; drive people to work faster; develop bad relationships. **Lean**: Completed unit of work must immediately move to the next step; make efforts to connect processes; improve information flow and make work easier.

Conventional: Don't need to know details of value-creating processes (courses and academic programs); stay in office and discuss problems third-hand in meetings; no understanding of value-added and waste and focus on people. **Lean**: Need to know the details of value-creating processes (courses and academic programs); visit academic units often to see problems first-hand; understand value-added and waste and focus on processes.

Conventional: People understand what management says; stop asking questions, speak in abstract terms. **Lean**: People do not understand what management says; ask questions; speak in specific terms.

Conventional: What gets measured gets managed; create many conflicting measures; measures are assumed to be accurate and helpful. **Lean**: What gets measured may not get managed [4]; use as few measures as possible; periodically evaluate measures for usefulness.
Conventional: Need data to manage; make data-driven decisions; make many poor decisions. **Lean**: Need data and facts to manage; make fact-based decisions; make many good decisions.

Conventional: Resources are scarce; maintain internal focus; ineffectively use resources. **Lean**: The amount of waste, unevenness, and unreasonableness is large; find and eliminate waste, unevenness, and unreasonableness; create resources by improving processes.

Conventional: Some things must be fixed; narrow use of problem-solving tools; make one-time fix and move on; **Lean**: Everything can be improved; broad-based use of continuous improvement processes, methods, and tools; continuous improvement.

Conventional: Employees are a cost; minimize employee costs; cut labor and benefits. **Lean**: Employees are valuable resources; treat employees fairly; hire and train carefully.

Conventional: What I learned in school (or on the job) is correct; defend knowledge areas, practices and results; perpetuate use of ineffective practices and not receptive to new ideas. **Lean**: What I learned in school (or on the job) may not be correct; seek new knowledge areas, new practices, and new results; develop innovative practices and be receptive to new ideas.

Conventional: Problems are bad; avoid problems; poor problem-solving capabilities. **Lean**: Problems are good; recognize and respond to problems rapidly; apply countermeasures to eliminate or reduce frequency of problem.

Conventional: Employees are well utilized; limit employee development; underutilize employees. **Lean**: Employees are greatly underutilized; work with employees to develop skills and capabilities; more fully utilize employees.

Conventional: Employees are respected; possess narrow view of respect; ensure employee time (and life) are wasted doing busy work. **Lean**: People must be respected; eliminate wasted human time and effort (to allow greater contribution); ensure meaningful work by increasing value.

Conventional: We do a good job educating students; do not question how students are educated; deliver to students less education than they could get. **Lean**: We may not be doing a good job educating students; understand and improve processes used to educate students; deliver education to students that improves over time.

On this last item, I would like digress to note that the teaching work that the faculty does is responsible for a large portion of university revenue (tuition and related fees). It is a very important activity, more than just for the revenue it generates. Teaching is central to the university's purpose, yet most presidents, provosts, deans and department chairs never enter the classroom to see how teachers teach. Therefore, they are useless when it comes to providing suggestions on how to improve and to help determine what types of support teachers ("the producers") might need to help them improve.

Lean leaders would never do this. They care greatly about the people and processes that define the organization's purpose and generate a large portion of the revenue. They would regularly enter the classroom to quietly and carefully observe. Through practice, they would develop an eye for detail and be non-blaming and non-judgmental in their feedback. They would focus on identifying process problems. (Note: Do not copy the complex K-12 teacher observation/evaluation rubrics. Their approach is both crazy and anti-Lean; they focus on blaming teachers and public humiliation [5]. Leaders must learn to observe and think for themselves).

For example, if a teacher cannot teach well, then an administrator has three choices: ignore the problem, blame the teacher, or recognize that the process for developing teaching skills in your university must be improved. Ignoring the problem yields no improvement. Blaming the teacher yields no improvement. Responsible leaders improve the process, and they allocate resources to prove they are serious about improvement – and serious about student engagement, graduation rates, and post-graduation student success.

Returning to the differences in beliefs, behaviors, and competencies between conventional (batch-and-queue) leaders and Lean (flow) leaders, I hope you can see that Lean beliefs, behaviors, and competencies reflect far more practical views of business than the views possessed by conventional leaders. Ignoring problems, for example, is impractical. While conventional leaders may have good hearts and good intentions, they possess beliefs that result in frustrated followers who feel they have much more to contribute. I have never met an employee who felt they were fully or effectively utilized at work. At best, they say they are utilized 50 percent. They want to do more, provided what they do matters. They do not want more meaningless busy work.

Much of the difference between conventional leaders and Lean leaders is in their ability or inability to avoid decision-making traps and illogical thinking. Specifically, the processes leaders engage in that either strengthen or weaken their susceptibility to decision-making traps and illogical thinking. The most common decision-making traps include [6]:

- Anchoring – Giving disproportionate weight to the first information received.
- Status Quo – Preference for solutions that preserve the current state.
- Sunk Cost – Make decisions that support past decisions.
- Confirming Evidence – Seek information that supports your viewpoint and ignore that which does not.
- Framing – Making decisions based on how a question or problem is framed.
- Estimating and Forecasting – Making estimates or forecasts for uncertain events.
- Overconfidence – Believing estimates or forecasts are accurate.
- Prudence – Adjusting estimates or forecasts to "be on the safe side."
- Recallability – Predictions of the future based on memory of past events.

The most common forms of illogical thinking include [7]:

- Denying the Antecedent: If A then B; Not A therefore, Not B.
- Affirming the Consequent: If A then B; B therefore, A.

- False Assumptions: Knowing or suspecting the assumption is false but using it anyway.
- Using and Abusing Tradition: Using tradition to argue against something.
- Ad hominem: Attack the person, not the argument.
- Avoiding the Force of Reason: Make false claims, obfuscate, mischaracterize, or use power to avoid confronting someone's argument.
- Abuse of Expertise: Using expertise or experts to justify an action.
- Red Herring: Divert someone's attention from the problem at hand.
- Inability to Disprove Does not Prove: Claiming to be correct because someone cannot prove you to be wrong.
- False Dilemma: Persuading people there are only two choices when there are many.
- Special Pleading: Omitting key information because it would undermine my position.
- Expediency: Ignoring the means to achieve a desired end.

These simply reflect the human condition; despite best efforts, we make many mistakes. The mistakes, however, can have severe consequences when made by people in leadership positions, and are exacerbated in highly political organizations. Politics creates vast amounts of waste, unevenness, and unreasonableness, and disables flow. In such organizations, decision-making traps and illogical thinking are assured – every hour, every day, every week, every month, and every year.

While we may think of leadership as intelligent, thoughtful, and capable, it would be wise to recognize it as an error-prone activity whose quality is normally very poor.

Kaizen is simply a process for applying the scientific method, and thus helps minimize or overcome decision-making traps and illogical thinking. So does the plan-do-check-act (PDCA) cycle, in addition to other Lean processes, methods, and tools. It is very important to understand their purpose and intent, and to use Lean processes, methods, and tools correctly. If not, you will fail to eliminate decision traps and illogical thinking, likely compounding your problems. In other words, efforts to improve will result in little or no improvement; waste, unevenness, and unreasonableness will grow.

We have again seen how leadership changes in three important ways: different beliefs, behaviors, and competencies; personal participation in process improvement; and recognition of and conscious efforts to avoid decision-making traps and eliminate illogical thinking.

Many leaders will say, "I don't have the time to learn something new." It is more likely that they do not want to learn anything new. If that is the case, then step aside. Leaders who are serious about improvement make the time. They eliminate some meetings; they improve meeting processes; they tell fewer long-winded stories; they delegate more effectively, etc. They do not filibuster improvement.

Is that all there is too it? No, there are other important ways in which leadership changes [8]. The following are typical characteristics of effective Lean leaders, all of which are learned through daily practice and exposure to different work experiences. This is not intended to be a complete list, but rather to give you a substantive idea:

- Reads and studies: A life-long learner. Wants to try out what they have learned.
- Curious: Likes to experiment and try new things. Not afraid to get their hands dirty.
- Asks why: Questions everything; especially conventional wisdom.
- Modest and unassuming: Not showy. Never says, "I already know that" or "I'm beyond that."
- Observes: Carefully observes people and processes. Focuses on process and results.

- Personally involved: Learns by doing and leads by example (servant leader).
- Persistent: Failure is not a barrier. Failure is a learning opportunity.
- Never stops thinking: Problems are a personal challenge.
- Never stops communicating: Likes to listen and teach others.
- Consistent: Devoted to development of self and others. Lots of personal discipline.
- Digs into things: Wants to understand problems, details, root causes, etc., using structured processes.
- Non-blaming, non-judgmental: Realizes that blaming and judging people is waste.
- Supportive: Likes to help people. Sets people up to succeed. Does not think people are the problem.
- Pragmatic: Alert to problems caused by management certitude and overconfidence.

Please be aware that Lean is a big personal challenge for leaders, most of whom have great difficulty with it. Lean management is easy to practice incorrectly [9].

Changing leadership will help improve two very important things: time and information flow.

Actual Time   ## University Time

First, it will more closely align university time with actual time, enabling the institution to compete better against other institutions. This will be due in part to more timely decision-making that is the result of better information flow which contains more accurate information.

Think about time and information flow in role as a leader. It is to cause delays (queues) and block information flow, or is it to eliminate time delays and improve information flow?

Here is an example of the logic of how Lean leaders think about improvement and about people:

This Is The Way Of Great Lean Leaders

Continuous Improvement Requires Respect for People

Respect for People Requires Having a Process Focus

Having a Process Focus Requires Thinking and Analysis

Thinking and Analysis Requires Asking Why

Asking Why Requires Curiosity

Curiosity Requires Humility

Humility Means Not Thinking You Know it All

Reminder: If you find yourself saying: "I already know that," don't listen.

Notes

[1] It has been interesting to witness some academic accreditation bodies move from being process-focused to results-focused. This is a huge mistake. Accreditation standards should be focused on both process and results. It would be even better if universities used accreditation standards as a guide or starting point instead of a requirement, because they tend to drag everyone toward the mean. Doing the things this book recommends would exceed any accreditation standard.

[2] M.L. Emiliani, "Linking Leaders' Beliefs to Their Behaviors and Competencies," *Management Decision*, Volume 41, No. 9, 2003, pp. 893-910

[3] M.L. Emiliani and D. Stec, "Using Value Stream Maps to Improve Leadership," *Leadership and Organizational Development Journal*, Volume 25, No. 8, 2004, pp. 622-645

[4] M.L. Emiliani, "The False Promise of 'What Gets Measured Gets Managed'," *Management Decision*, Vol. 38, No. 9, 2000, pp. 612-615

[5] K-12 educators in the U.S. should adopt Lean management as well, in part to reverse the reprehensible culture of blame. See B. Stecher and S. Kirby, *Organizational Improvement and Accountability: Lessons for Education from Other Sectors*, Rand Corporation, Arlington, VA, 2004 and Betty Ziskovsky's Lean Education Enterprises.

[6] J.S. Hammond, R.L. Keeney, and H. Raiffa, "The Hidden Traps in Decision Making," *Harvard Business Review*, September-October 1998, Vol. 76, No. 5, pp. 47-52

[7] D.Q. McInerny, *Being Logical: A Guide to Good Thinking*, Random House, New York, NY, 2005

[8] M.L. Emiliani, "Standardized Work for Executive Leadership," *Leadership and Organizational Development Journal*, Vol. 29, No. 1, 2008, pp. 24-46

[9] M.L. Emiliani and D.J. Stec, "Leaders Lost in Transformation," *Leadership and Organizational Development Journal*, Vol. 26, No. 5, 2005, p. 370-387.

4

Gaining Buy-In

Conventional management can be characterized as relying on the heroic work of key individuals and managers directing employees on what to do and when to do it. Where this occurs, broad-based employee buy-in may not be necessary in order to create a plan or achieve some of the plan's goals. The risk is that employees may not agree with the plan and work to undermine its execution.

Lean management is different. The management system asks for everyone's participation; for employees to think for themselves rather than wait to be told what to do. This does not mean employees do anything what they want to do. Instead, it means that the leadership team establishes strategy and direction (based on reality, not whim), and employees engage in identifying and correcting the myriad problems that occur along the way. Employees are empowered to eliminate waste, unevenness, and unreasonableness using Lean principles and practices without having to seek management's permission.

Thus, broad-based employee buy-in is critical to the daily successful practice of Lean. This means many things with respect to what leaders can and cannot do, as you will learn in this chapter.

University leaders with a "my-way-or-the-highway" approach to their leadership will immediately fail with Lean. Why? Because nothing has changed. These types of leaders call for Lean management, but they will continue to lead as they did before in their conventional, zero-sum ways. The leadership style and the management system are at odds.

Instead, the "my-way-or-the-highway" leaders will have to modify their behaviors significantly to align themselves with the Lean management system [1]. Most will not be able to do this. They are deeply committed to the behaviors that inhibit information flow, dis-empower people, and threaten people. The only context they can conceive of Lean is one in which it is mean. These zero-sum behaviors include:

- Bullying
- Autocratic
- Blame
- Public humiliation
- Office politics
- Condescending
- Micro-managing
- Cannot admit errors
- Retaliation
- Unknown expectations
- Centralized decision-making
- Ego mania

These types of behaviors entrench batch-and-queue information processing in the university and create huge delays in action. They help ensure employees keep quiet when problems arise, anemic teamwork, and a dearth of creative and innovative ideas for improving processes. These leadership behaviors force employees to focus on individual survival rather than organizational success. They harm other stakeholders as well. In short, being an asshole generates mountains of behavioral waste, which is inconsistent with the "Respect for People" principle in Lean management.

In contrast, Lean leaders behave in ways that facilitate information flow and enable people to improve their work every day. After all, leaders asking workers to eliminate waste, unevenness, and unreasonableness must behave in ways that are consistent with that request. It makes sense that if I ask workers to eliminate waste in business processes, then I cannot behave in ways that create waste in business or leadership processes [2]. Instead, Lean leaders have to exhibit value-added behaviors.

Value-added leadership behaviors are the types of behaviors that energize and engage people. These behaviors motivate them to want to learn new things and participate in daily improvement activities. The value-added, non-zero-sum leadership behaviors that enable people to improve and facilitate information flow include:

- Humility
- Calmness
- Listening
- Trust
- Reflection
- Honesty
- Gratitude
- Consistency
- Patience
- Humor
- Objectivity
- Wisdom
- Observation
- Balance

These leadership behaviors are obviously consistent with the "Respect for People" principle and will promote daily continuous improvement. Recall: "It ceases to be Lean management the moment it is used for bad." Lean is not mean.

The university must formally adopt a policy that states:

> "No employee shall be unemployed as a result of
> participating in kaizen (continuous improvement).
> Jobs may change, but new roles and responsibilities
> will be negotiated to achieve mutually beneficial,
> non-zero-sum outcomes."

This policy will help enormously in gaining employee buy-in. However, management must be very careful not to associate continuous improvement with any job losses that may occur due to poor economic conditions – either in fact or in perception. Failure to do so will kill buy-in. If you mess this up, as so many manufacturing business leaders have done in the last 30 years, you will send the dispiriting message to employees that no matter how well you do, you will lose.

Faculty and staff will buy-in to Lean management more easily if they understand that they will not be harmed by it. And, as noted, buy-in will be stronger and occur more quickly when employees see their leaders participating in improvement activities individually and as regular team members.

Let's say you did everything correctly, yet many faculty members remain skeptical and truly believe that Lean management is fine for administrative work, but totally inappropriate for academic work. As you know, their feedback may be more confrontational than it is diplomatic. Lean leaders would look past the confrontational delivery and instead look for its deeper meaning.

The Lean leader would ask probing questions to determine the source of the resistance, partly out of curiosity. Also, they would reason that for every faculty member who speaks up, there are many others who share the same concerns but will not speak up. Thus, Lean leaders would see this is as a good thing: an opportunity to solve a problem and learn. If you can find the causes of the effect that you are seeing, then you have an opportunity to expand faculty buy-in. What you learn will be useful in the future, as there will surely be new faculty (or staff or administrators) who will be similarly skeptical.

Faculty (or anyone else's) feedback critical of Lean may come up in meetings, where it is extremely important to handle it in ways that are perceived as respectful of their concerns. There will be a lot of one-on-one interaction between leaders and faculty to resolve questions and concerns. Importantly, Lean leaders would never ask faculty to come to their offices to discuss problems because it reinforces the power relationship that exists between managers and workers and diminishes bilateral learning. Instead, Lean leaders go to where the people are to see things with their own eyes, ascertain facts, and ask questions in a non-blaming, non-judgmental way. Faculty and staff critical of Lean will express concerns that, when understood deeply, will fall into one or more of these categories:

- De-humanize them.
- Speed them up and burn them out.
- De-skill them.
- Take away their knowledge.
- Take away their creativity.
- Cost them their job.

They want to know: "What's in it for me?" From their perspective, you have probably done little or nothing that they would recognize as having made their job easier or removed burdens – perhaps for decades. Managers usually pile additional requirements on employees (and department chairs) and never take anything away. So how are things different now?

You will explain the benefits of Lean management in general, and how strategy deployment [3] in particular is providing needed focus so that people work on what matters most. Lean management should have the effect of improving work and working conditions; to humanize the workplace. If not, you are doing something wrong.

It is likely that faculty, in particular (as well as lower-level university leaders), will ask to see evidence of success before they buy-in. They will want to know where Lean management has worked in a university, in academics. Nearly everyone who is unfamiliar with Lean seeks this type of information. Their desire ranges from honest inquiry to a stalling tactic to avoid having to learn anything new or do anything different. First, recognize that even if you provide ironclad proof, many people will find other excuses for not buying-in. There is no one example or answer that will satisfy everyone and immediately result in 100 percent buy-in. You have to work at it.

Second, any inability to prove that Lean can be applied to teaching does not disprove it can work. Lean works wherever information is processed and exchanged. Everyone thinks they are different, as Morris Cooke noted in 1910. The fact is, there have only been few examples of Lean principles and practices applied to teaching in higher education [4, 5, 6]. Faculty should use these as examples to get them started in their own daily application of Lean principles and practices. University leaders will have to challenge, motivate, and educate faculty through facts, dialog, persuasion, visits to other organizations practicing Lean management, and so on.

Third, despite faculty being highly educated, they will do what most people do: throw up many illogical arguments in an attempt to maintain the status quo. You can expect emotional arguments as well. Some faculty will be offended at the thought that others might view their work as inferior, or they will resist the idea that their work can be improved.

To ease their pain and to influence change as a condition of buy-in, some administrators, faculty, and staff, will want to modify Lean management by cherry-picking the good parts, or changing the names of various Lean methods or tools. Kaizen becomes "rapid improvement event," "kaizen blitz," "Lean event," and so on, thus losing its original meaning (i.e. kaizen is a daily activity, not a sporadic event).

They will also try to reduce improvement opportunities to very thin slices so that little of their time is consumed and the change made is not significant. All you have is the appearance of buy-in and continuous improvement. For example, instead of a team-based kaizen resulting in the improvement of several important things, kaizen becomes atomized so that people work on improving only one small thing. These are the wrong things to do, and leadership should not allow this.

Faculty will also surely want to know how improvement activities fit into evaluation criteria and in their annual evaluation process. For faculty, kaizen should count as service. In keeping with Lean thinking, the ratio of the evaluation criteria – teaching, research, and service – should not be fixed. The ratios should be changeable each semester or every year, as dictated by the needs of the faculty member, department, school, or university. This way, you avoid the impression that participation in kaizen is work that must be done "in addition to" other duties.

A faculty member who is highly engaged in kaizen and wants to become a team leader might, for one year, have teaching, research, and service contribution of 20 percent, zero percent, 80 percent instead of the usual 50 percent, 40 percent, 10 percent. The ratios should be floating, not fixed.

In many universities, the ratios stated in faculty handbooks do not reflect reality for promotion and tenure. Service contribution, for example, may need to be much more than 10 percent and research more than 40 percent, while teaching remains 50 percent (but is usually lightly regarded and considered "a given"). This reflects the existence of both unevenness and unreasonableness, and indicates the need for kaizen to assure faculty workloads reflect reality. In addition, Lean thinking suggests that faculty workload categories should be changed to teaching, research, and *improvement*.

Another aspect of gaining buy-in relates to improving how faculty are evaluated by students and their peers. In the case of student evaluation, there is probably substantial opportunity for improvement in most universities. For example, a university may use evaluation forms that contain 20 or more questions on a one-to-five scale, plus a place to write in comments. The evaluation is complex and lengthy, so many students will give high scores just to cut short the time it takes to give feedback. The outcome is one in which feedback is highly variable and not very specific or actionable for faculty members. In addition, many faculty members ignore the feedback and there is no mechanism for accountability.

This is a process ripe for kaizen. The result would be a process that is simpler and yields better information for faculty, coupled with a commitment by faculty to act upon the feedback for every course taught. It could be as simple as a half-page form containing a course rating scale of A-B-C-D-F (circle one), with three spaces for identifying what students liked about the course and three suggestions for how the course can be improved. It would also contain a faculty rating scale of A-B-C-D-F (circle one), with three spaces for feedback on what the teacher did well and three suggestions for how teaching can be improved. The suggestions should be collected (anonymously), shared among faculty in a given department or school, and acted upon to the greatest extent possible. Whatever you do, it must be simple and practical; do not create new burdens.

Likewise, the normally laborious and time-consuming promotion and tenure processes can be greatly improved using kaizen to help assure that it is based on merit, and that the faculty workload categories are consistently and correctly evaluated. In both cases, kaizen for these processes should be ongoing activities, not one-time events.

It would also be helpful if universities that adopt Lean also adopt the Caux Roundtable *Principles for Responsible Business* [7]. The Principles for Responsible Business are fully consistent with the Lean management system, and can help develop a common perspective among stakeholders. It will also assist with gaining buy-in for Lean by helping faculty recognize that the fundamental desire and intent is to do good things. That must be the actual outcome.

If improvement is seen as a burden or a threat, then faculty will not buy-in and participate. In universities where this happens, they will find what so many organizations in the private sector have found: Management can mandate participation in improvement, but little in the way of actual improvement will be achieved. Improvement will become politicized and people will play games to give the appearance of improvement.

The challenge for a university leader is to learn something new and to concurrently provide new learning opportunities for faculty and staff. Learn Lean management together, as a team, from books, by speaking to people, on-the-job participation in improvement activities, and so on. Make Lean fun and people will come.

We must face the fact that most undergraduate students, after taking 40 courses, will a few years after graduation say something like: "Yeah, I had 3 or 4 good professors, and I still remember what they taught me. The rest I can't really remember." This is a terrible outcome. We know the processes lead to this result. If such a statement does not suggest there are enormous opportunities for improvement in higher education, then what does?

Academic processes cannot be improved without faculty. Therefore, it is critical to gain their buy-in. As professionals, faculty should want to improve their own work and participate in kaizen teams to help others improve their work. Yet some, perhaps many, faculty members will declare tenure as the rationale for their ability to refuse to participate. Those faculty members must be reminded that tenure means they have been awarded academic freedom to teach, conduct research, and publish their results free of obstruction and free of retaliation by their employer. Tenure does not confer the right to faculty to decline reasonable requests by their employer to participate in processes to improve the quality and value of services that the university offers.

Process improvement does not have an agenda to interfere with academic freedom. If such were the case then kaizen will have been greatly misunderstood and misapplied, and administration should bear the full force of any consequences.

In the kaizens that I led at Rensselaer Polytechnic Institute in 2002 and 2003, the issue of academic freedom never came up. The faulty who participated in kaizen saw no relationship between honest, collegial efforts to improve teaching and academic freedom.

It seems inevitable that some tenured faculty will rebel in one fuktosecond (10^{-69} s) [8]. This is to be expected in organizations where employees have historically enjoyed enormous latitude in the work they do and unbridled personal freedoms (as distinct from academic freedom). Much good come comes from this arrangement, but some bad too. The bad will aggressively surface if university leadership is not very careful in how they present Lean management to faculty. Be very careful, and have a good plan.

Notes

[1] M.L. Emiliani, "Lean Behaviors," *Management Decision*, Vol. 36, No. 9, 1998, pp. 615-631

[2] Most people do not understand leadership from a process perspective. Leaders and followers perceive leadership to be an ad hoc assortment of daily activities, even when the specific roles and responsibilities of leaders are fairly well-defined. Variation in leadership processes from one manager to another contributes greatly to perceptions of poor leadership. The process perspective improves people's comprehension of leadership and also helps them realize that leadership is not the domain of the few people who possess unique personal characteristics such as charisma. Almost anyone can become an effective Lean leader. The process perspective also helps people to do a better job of evaluating leadership quality and effectiveness.

[3] M. Cowley and E. Domb, *Beyond Strategic Vision: Effective Corporate Action with Hoshin Planning*, Butterworth-Heinemann, New York, NY, 1997

[4] M.L. Emiliani, "Improving Business School Courses by Applying Lean Principles and Practices," *Quality Assurance in Education*, Vol. 12, No. 4, 2004, pp. 175-187

[5] M.L. Emiliani, "Using Kaizen to Improve Graduate Business School Degree Programs," *Quality Assurance in Education*, Vol. 13, No. 1, 2005, pp. 37-52

[6] M.L. Emiliani, "Team Leader's Kaizen Manual For Academic Courses and Programs," unpublished work, 2002 (updated 2009, 2012, and 2013).

[7] "Principles for Responsible Business," Caux Round Table, Washington., D.C., May 2010

[8] Goodbye attosecond (10^{-18} s). The author has determined through elaborate and painstaking experiments that this is the exact length of time that it takes tenured full professors to get annoyed with administrators. It is thought to be a fundamental physical constant of nature, such as the speed of light. This incredible discovery has been named the "Emiliani constant" in honor of the renowned geologist Dr. Cesare Emiliani (1922-1995), renaissance scientist and raconteur, who predicted that the number

of university administrators would become infinite by the year 2023 (C. Emiliani, "Doomsyear 2023," *J. Irreproducible Results*, Vol. 33, No. 5, p. 9, May/June 1988).

5

Individual Participation

This chapter will focus on what faculty (full time and part-time) can do to improve their own work. The same ideas, however, apply to all staff and administrators. Much of the work (information processing) that faculty members do is completely within their control. Faculty are professionals, who, like all professionals, seek to make fewer errors over time by developing their skills and capabilities. However, this does not generally seem to be the case in higher education, where problems related to teaching can linger uncorrected for years.

For example, many faculty members lovingly carry forward traditions in teaching that pissed them off when they were students. If you did not like something when you were a student, then why would you do you do it to others as a teacher? Would you not instead think deeply about the merits of the tradition? Can it be improved? Is it even necessary?

One such tradition pertains to testing. Students like to work and learn, but most do not like tests. That begs the question: Which courses actually need testing in the traditional sense, and which do not? After all, higher education is optional education, not required education. So the structure and norms pertaining to K-12 education need not apply. We can be creative and innovative in our efforts to ensure learning objectives are achieved with requisite academic rigor. Why not do that?

The assumption is that tests are needed to evaluate student learning. The better assumption is that evaluation of student learning is needed, and testing is just one approach. The test that many faculty members administer is in-class mid-term and final exams. From my perspective as a Lean thinker, this is the worst way to evaluate student learning.

Teachers hate grading and so they minimize testing to twice per semester, for example. That is the tradition; it is done for the convenience of the professor, not for the benefit of students. From the Lean perspective, mid-term and final exams represent two large batches of information that sit in queue for a long period of time until they are processed and moved to the next step. Students usually receive their graded exam weeks later, resulting in feedback that is decoupled from when the test was given. The delay renders the test result meaningless to many students because they have moved on to other things. And, of course, a test that carries 50 percent of the grade means that students' study efforts will focus on passing the test, not on learning the material and understanding it in ways that may be relevant to their lives.

From students' perspective, these exams are a big mistake. They do not like their grade for the course based on two exams, and the structure of the evaluation denies many students the opportunity to actually learn. Professors, focused on their perspective of teaching, evaluation, and tradition, do not see it that way.

Lean people are always focused on being practical and thinking deeply about what works well for a given situation (i.e. minimum of waste, unevenness, and unreasonableness) – but which may have to be improved as things change over time. There could indeed be some courses where some formulation of mid-term and final exams makes sense and also achieves the desired learning outcomes for students. However, this would be unusual.

It is more likely that to achieve the desired learning outcomes for students, faculty have to do things that are less convenient for them but much better for students. For example, faculty have only 40 or so classroom hours to impart explicit as well as important tacit knowledge to students. Why waste precious class time by giving in-class tests? That means professors, instead of being idle during in-class-tests, have more time to teach during each semester.

A Lean faculty member would first work to determine what is it that students must learn from the course that will help them in their personal and work lives, and enrich them as human beings. This would be identified as the most important material in the course. There would be an ongoing process of continuous improvement to refine what is considered most important because things change over time and with feedback. This, in turn, informs the modes of student evaluation.

Consistent with Lean, the professor would seek to reduce the batch sizes of information given to students and reduce the number of duration queues to enable more frequent processing of information and more timely feedback. They would think about 4 tests per semester, 6 tests per semester, and so on. Ultimately, the professor would decide to give short, focused weekly assignments that are submitted the day before class, evaluated, and then discussed in class the next day. Assignment question(s) would be carefully crafted to focus students' attention on the desired learning outcomes for each week and for the course, and emphasize processing the information they absorbed.

A Lean faculty member would also look to determine if other modes of evaluation used add unnecessary complexity to the course and cause a loss of focus among students. Are there opportunities to simplify grading while improving learning outcomes? Is the grading subjective and therefore less meaningful; e.g. class participation (how do you fairly grade introverts)? Are students put on teams simply because that is the thing to do? If the students are working professionals, are they put on teams to complete assignments? Why do that when they are subject to teamwork every day at work? Will the university teamwork experience do anything for them?

Another tradition is to overwhelm students with reading material. Is all of that reading really necessary, or does much of it amount to unfocused busy-work. Are lengthy term papers required because that is the tradition? Do assigned projects really enforce the learning? The Lean faculty member would think about these and many more things, and would use the plan-do-check-act (PDCA) cycle every day to improve their work.

My own viewpoint is: "Don't piss off students." Why? Is it because they are customers? No. It is because most students who are angry with the instructor will forget what they were taught and immediately move on to the next thing. This outcome diminishes the value of higher education even if students did have more than 3 or 4 good professors out of 40. In addition, it is disrespectful to piss off students and therefore inconsistent with Lean principles.

Here are 45 ways that teachers anger students (in no particular order):

- Cannot teach.
- Does not know the material.
- Cannot answer questions.
- Gets frustrated when students ask questions.
- Cannot explain the material.
- Comes to class unprepared.
- Goes too fast.
- Reads from the book.
- Fails to add teacher's knowledge or perspective to a topic.
- Fails to engage class in the discussion.
- Fails to use teaching technologies.
- Style remains stagnant for 25 years.
- Does not use real-world examples.
- Frequently changes book or edition.
- Requires a big expensive book, then does not use it.
- Habitually late to class.
- Class runs past end time.
- Talks about themselves or tell life stories that are irrelevant.
- Explains topic only one way.
- Tenured teachers who don't care or give up.
- Randomly teaching different topics.
- Not communicating what students are expected to know.
- Required courses that assume extensive background or prior knowledge.

- Bases entire grade on 2 or 3 exams.
- Attendance does not count as part of the grade.
- Does little more than show lots of PowerPoint slides.
- Ignores student feedback.
- Acts in vengeful ways.
- Coursework is different than the syllabus.
- Gives poor assignment work instructions.
- Ambiguous assignment work instructions.
- Actual grading does not reflect grading on syllabus.
- Poor feedback on projects and presentations.
- Professor acknowledges complexity of a topic or assignment but fails to explain it to students.
- Many cancelled classes (and sometimes not telling students).
- Too much PowerPoint.
- Too many videos.
- Insufficient classroom activities.
- Use of outdated teaching materials.
- Testing that is not responsive to student's individual strengths; e.g. multiple choice vs. essay (essay being the way some students would prefer to answer test questions).
- Standing in queue outside of professor's office to get help.
- Pop quizzes.
- Professors who say: "You should drop the course, but I'll still be teaching it next semester."
- Professors who say: "I'm not here to teach you. That's your job. I'm here to test you."
- Speaking to students in condescending ways.

There seems to be a problem here.

People in higher education often struggle to define quality. Based on these 45 problems, let's start with this simple definition (which can be improved upon over time): "Quality is the absence of known or obvious defects."

These 45 known defects indicate significant process problems exist
that must be improved, such as: hiring, training for classroom (and
online) teaching, faculty evaluation, promotion and tenure, and
management controls. But remember, do not blame the people;
blame the process. Blaming people will leave these teaching and
process problems forever unaddressed.

Top administrators always say something like "students come
first." The rhetoric does not match the reality. Students do not
come first. And leadership has failed. An important takeaway is
that the faculty who are substantially free of these 45 problems are
regarded by administrators as equivalent in teaching capability to
those faculty who are substantially encumbered by these 45
problems. Good quality teaching is the same as bad quality
teaching. How can that be? This is another failure by leaders, who
have obviously been working on many of the wrong things.

One does not have to think of students as customers to realize that
these are long-standing, fundamental problems that must be
corrected. University leaders habitually ignore the lack of quality
and continuous improvement in teaching, and then typically join
others in blaming faculty for teaching problems (i.e. "Remove the
bad teachers!"). In contrast, Lean leaders accept responsibility; they
do not blame faculty; they do not make excuses about unions,
tenure, etc.; and they work with people to improve. They make the
time to do that because it helps fulfill the university's purpose.

It is telling that the students who pay tuition themselves are often
quite vocal in their feedback about these problems. They want to
receive higher quality services for the money that they pay out of
their own pockets (vs. parents or employer or pockets).
Universities have been able to avoid scrutiny in the past because
the student and the payer are usually different persons, so the
feedback on value proposition is not as sharp. The students who
pay their own tuition can offer some of the highest fidelity
feedback. Professors will remain nameless, but the problems shall
be named. We must know about problems in order to improve.
Problems are good. The best managers have lots of problems.

Each one of the items listed represents major opportunities that, if corrected, would be recognized by students as improvements. Despite inactive leadership, every item is 100 percent under the control of individual faculty members. Each faculty member could do whatever they see fit to make corrections. However, that would lead to high levels of variation that might cause other problems.

The Lean management system teaches employees to be autonomous in identifying and correcting problems in their own work. With Lean management, individual professors would use similar methods to identify and correct problems. This assures consistency in the problem-solving process, resulting in more uniform outcomes. Students should see consistency in the courses in their major and across their degree program. This means that while faculty use similar methods to identify and correct problems, they should also be talking to one another about what they are doing to improve.

Let's assume most faculty correct the obvious big problems previously listed (a bad assumption). What about small problems? What about tiny problems? Is there commitment to improve one's work across the entire scale of problems, from giant to miniscule? Probably not. This means that problems that are insignificant to faculty, yet are significant to students, will likely go uncorrected – perhaps for one's entire teaching career.

Lean management teaches people to apply continuous improvement methods and tools to all problems, no matter how big or small. In practice, some routes to correcting problems may not be easy or even recognizable. Lean people do not ignore the problem because they cannot immediately correct it. Instead, they keep track of the problems visually, such as on a flip chart, so that they can continue to think about the problems and how they can be improved.

The approach to daily problem-solving in Lean management is unique and an important part of hands-on Lean training. Previous training in problem-solving that faculty have had may be helpful, but once again, with Lean, you are learning something new [1-4].

The fundamental perspective in Lean is that most problems (95 percent) can be understood relatively quickly and then rapidly acted upon. Other problems require the gathering of additional data and information, and greater analysis and thought. But to be very clear, Lean is action-oriented; meaning, understand the problem, identify root cases, and implement practical countermeasures to reduce the frequency of recurrence or eliminate the problem altogether. Lean is not the traditional approach to problem-solving where people study everything to death and take ages to actually accomplish something good. Lean is not committee work.

The teaching problems identified earlier reflect a cavalier attitude about students, teaching, learning, and one's own job. In particular, many teachers fail to see the once-in-a-lifetime opportunity that face-to-face teaching offers for imparting useful explicit and especially tacit knowledge to students. If we continue to ignore that opportunity, then students will, in the future, give greater consideration to the online degree programs offered by for-profit universities.

While not discounting any positive role the for-profits may play in higher education [5], the fact is that traditional not-for-profit universities, led for decades using status quo oriented conventional management, have a lot of work to do to improve. Much can be done by individual faculty, and even more can be done in teams. Both can work quickly and also be very effective, while improving academic rigor and value.

Make no mistake about it, higher education has long been a buyers' market, yet universities have acted as if it has been a sellers' market (e.g. non-stop tuition increases, poor teaching quality, etc.). The combination of for-profit universities and payers looking for better deals (government, parents, employers, etc.) are accelerating the need for university leaders to acknowledge the buyers' market they exist in and to rapidly improve their services and control costs far more effectively than they have in the past. Faculty will play a large role in making that happen. They will need to be flexible and begin to try new things [6, 7], and not disappear behind the cloak of tenure. It is a matter of being a little more humble and pitching in to make things better and better for everyone.

University leaders must not put faculty on a treadmill that increases workplace stress in the name of performance improvement [7]. Fewer problems should lead to lower stress and improved creativity and innovation.

Notes

[1] M.L. Emiliani, "Improving Business School Courses by Applying Lean Principles and Practices," *Quality Assurance in Education*, Vol. 12, No. 4, 2004, pp. 175-187

[2] J. Liker, *The Toyota Way*, McGraw-Hill, New York, NY, 2004. See page 256 for a diagram of Toyota's practical problem-solving process.

[3] J. Shook, *Managing to Learn: Using the A3 Management Process*, Lean Enterprise Institute, Cambridge, MA, 2008

[4] M. Rother, *Toyota Kata*, McGraw-Hill, New York, NY, 2010.

[5] The dearth of research coming from for-profit education institutions indicates they are better thought of as post-secondary private schools rather than universities. Higher education has historically recognized a role beyond simply teaching and awarding degrees.

[6] D. Berrett, "Harvard Conference Seeks to Jolt University Teaching," *Chronicle of Higher Education*, 5 February 2012

[7] L. Summers, "What You (Really) Need to Know," *The New York Times*, 20 January 2012

[7] The personal drive needed to obtain a terminal degree is often associated with persons who are studious and solitary. Large numbers of faculty are introverts. This may account for some of the teaching problems cited in this chapter. Most introverts enjoy solitary scholarship far more than classroom teaching because it requires them to do things that they are not comfortable doing. Introverts tend to be awkward in social settings and typically dislike being the center of attention. Leaders must be cautious in efforts to improve faculty's teaching skills (e.g. speaking, presentation, and discussion facilitating skills), as it could increase stress. Requiring in-class peer evaluation, videotaping faculty to critique their teaching style, etc., will be very off-putting to many professors and suggests the need to consider other solutions. This illustrates the importance of the "Respect for People" principle.

6

Team Participation

Like any organization, universities have unwritten pecking orders in which leaders view some departments or employees as more important than others. Employees will also view some departments and peers as more important than others. Legendary is the view among faculty that they are far more important than both staff and administrators. Thus, your university begins its improvement efforts from the long-standing position of disrespecting people. That has to change.

The fact is that to run a university you need different departments and people with different skills and capabilities. Universities need all of these to function properly (in alphabetical order):

- Academics
- Admissions
- Bookstore
- Facilities
- Finance
- Food Services
- Human Resources
- Information Technology
- Legal
- Library
- Marketing
- Medical
- Purchasing
- Registrar
- Public Safety, etc.

If certain people or departments are ignored, then we will fail to comprehend the university as a system and instead see it narrowly as discrete parts that must be individually optimized. In conventional management, efforts to improve work are compartmentalized so that no one person understands any process in its entirety. Everyone dutifully does their job, but the overall workflow is choppy and productivity is low. Marginalizing certain people or departments forces people to improve their work in isolation, which further supports batch-and-queue information processing.

With Lean management, we change our focus from results to process and results, and start to understand the importance of other people and other departments. We start to see the university as a system, much like the human body, where all the vital parts are needed for its successful functioning. Focusing on processes also helps us understand how information is transformed from one step to another, which helps us identify waste, unevenness, and unreasonableness. This, in turn, improves process quality and reliability and improves information flow. Batch sizes become smaller, and queues are fewer in number and shorter in duration.

The challenge is to understand and connect processes. To do that, people who possess knowledge of pieces of the process must come together to establish what the process is and then identify opportunities to improve the process. Improvement requires teamwork, yet the long-established pattern of favoring certain people or departments over others undercuts teamwork. The way to move away from that is through kaizen.

Kaizen, done right, helps humanize the workplace and improve cooperation, communication, and enthusiasm for work. Recall that kaizen means:

"Change for the better,"

For an improvement to qualify as an actual improvement, it must not negatively impact upstream or downstream processes or people. Nor can it negatively impact internal or external stakeholders. Kaizen must be non-zero-sum (win-win). Recall also three principles for kaizen:

- Process and results
- System focus
- Non-blaming, non-judgmental

Kaizen must be free of organizational politics to function effectively. The scientific method and politics are at odds with one another.

Kaizen teaches people how to recognize a problem, analyze a problem quickly, identify practical countermeasures, implement countermeasures, and measure and evaluate results.

Kaizen consists of six steps [1]:

1. Discover improvement potential.
2. Analyze current methods.
3. Generate ideas.
4. Develop an implementation plan.
5. Implement the plan.
6. Evaluate the new method.

People must be open-minded and use their creativity to identify no cost or low-cost solutions to problems. Kaizen teams should "spend ideas, not dollars" to solve problems. Sometimes dollars are needed, but far less so than you might imagine.

There are several forms of kaizen [2], including:

- Individual
- Small team, 2-6 people
- Large team, 10-20 people

Usually, the number of people involved increases as the scope of the process to be improved increases. Improving small portions of a process generally requires small teams, while improving large parts of a process generally requires larger teams. Large teams are always comprised of people from different departments. Small teams may be comprised of people from one or more departments depending on the problem.

In general, teams should be cross-functional and include people from the process to be improved as well as upstream and downstream personnel. The team should also include people who have no direct relationship to the process because, in addition to helping out, they invariably provide unique perspectives. Their lack of familiarity with the process (or subject matter) makes them expert at asking questions that others would never think to ask. Do not dismiss them.

Thus, kaizens to improve individual courses and academic programs should include:

• Faculty from different disciplines (full time and part time)
• Staff
• Administrators
• Alumni

It can also include people from industry, trustees, legislators, and other stakeholders.

Everyone who participates in team-based kaizen does so as a team member (other than the team leader), and not in their official university function. In other words, the president of the university, provost, vice presidents, etc., participate as regular team members. Roles, responsibilities, and rank outside of the kaizen team's activities are irrelevant. People in leadership positions must not act like leaders in kaizen teams, and will not usually serve as team leaders due to the ease with which their dual roles can confuse team members.

It is important to reiterate that everyone in the university must participate in kaizen, top to bottom, because this is how people learn Lean management. It is how they learn about processes and how to improve them, and how to improve their own work.

Nobody is exempt, not even finance and legal personnel. In addition, recognize that kaizen is a long-term learning process; identifying and eliminating waste, unevenness, and unreasonableness is a valuable skill acquired over time through repeated participation in kaizen.

Faculty accept peer review as a reasonably good process for improving the quality of their scholarship (but can also be greatly improved). Think of kaizen as a peer review process for improving teaching by improving individual courses and degree programs.

There are many ways in which kaizen can be ruined. Small errors in administrators' understanding of kaizen can lead to big problems. For example, kaizen is not a planning activity. The result of kaizen is actual improvement, not future plans for improvement. Also, kaizen teams are empowered to make improvement without having to ask management for permission. Kaizen teams work to eliminate waste, unevenness, and unreasonableness, and should have standing permission from top leaders to do just that. If management confuses kaizen with conventional management practices and attaches many reviews and approvals to it, or treats kaizen as "projects," then nothing will get done and kaizen will quickly die.

Kaizen must be understood and practiced correctly. That means, among other things, that team-based kaizen must not become atomized so that people work on improving only one small thing. Kaizen seeks to rapidly improve many things at once. This gives people a far greater feeling of accomplishment, which energizes and motivates people to do more kaizen. It also attracts people who have never experienced kaizen.

In addition, at the conclusion of kaizen, there should be few or no outstanding action items. All action items should be completed during the kaizen. In cases where the action items cannot be completed, the additional time needed should be realistic and not padded. The kaizen team leader must follow-up on any outstanding action items to assure their completion.

Here are some other important tips for ensuring kaizen is correctly applied:

- Administrators' role is to advocate kaizen, budget for kaizen, identify kaizen opportunities, select team members, support teams, participate, in kaizen teams, and learn.

- Administrators practice the three principles of kaizen, and their involvement must be consistent with the two Lean principles "Continuous Improvement" and "Respect for People."

- Kaizen teams establish improvement targets, while the kaizen facilitator adjusts the improvement targets up or down – not management.

- Administrators support kaizen teams. They do not criticize or second guess.

- Administrators do not steer or politicize kaizen.

- Administrators attend daily kaizen close-out meetings to show support, learn, share, plan, and to demonstrate the "Respect for People" principle.

Detailed descriptions of how to apply kaizen for academic programs have been described elsewhere [3, 4]. University leaders, faculty, and staff should carefully read these papers.

The kaizens that I facilitated in higher education were seen by faculty and staff as a very positive experience. Faculty benefitted from having others review their courses in a non-blaming and non-judgmental way. Team members stick to the facts and provide information to the teacher that they could not have obtained by themselves. Faculty gain a better understanding of what they are trying to accomplish in their courses, and the changes made better align with student expectations and the desired learning outcomes.

Kaizen gives faculty, staff, administrators, and alumni an opportunity to interact together in ways that that they have not done before. Faculty who participate in kaizen as team members will be energized to incorporate improvements in their courses, even if their courses are not the subject of any future kaizen. Kaizen generates many new ideas for current and future use.

Kaizen is not without problems. There will be faculty who feel threatened, especially when senior administrators are present as kaizen team members. Feeling threatened is not the intent of kaizen. This situation can be improved by clearly communicating to faculty the objectives of kaizen and communicating to senior administrators that they must be seen as team members and not as the boss.

Another opportunity for improvement pertains to the daily kaizen close-out meetings. Administrators, in particular, must show interest in kaizen and attend the daily close-out meetings. Low participation in these brief meetings will be perceived by kaizen team members as a lack of interest from management. This diminishes team members' desire to participate in future kaizens. Management participation helps fulfill the intent of the daily close-out meeting, which is to brief people – any employee – on the improvements that were made. Broader participation results in additional suggestions for improvement and demonstrates management commitment to kaizen.

The strength of people's desire to continuously improve affects the results achieved in kaizen. Faculty must be willing to improve, and the facilitator and team members – faculty, staff, administrators, and alumni – must be willing to challenge each other in non-threatening ways towards the goal of improvement. Kaizen, explained and applied correctly, works in academic settings because it encourages thoughtful dialog, introduces faculty to a new structured process for inquiry, promotes cross-functional teamwork, and identifies specific actions that faculty can take to quickly improve their courses.

Academic organizations are like any other organization in that it can be difficult to obtain broad-based participation in formal process improvement activities – especially when the tools or methods are unfamiliar, and faculty are not certain if administrators truly support the activity. In addition, faculty tend to have low regard for anything that comes from industry; that it will somehow conflict with the purpose of the institution or the traditions of academia. The educated must be far more discriminating than that and not proffer illogical arguments (e.g. denying the antecedent) to avoid doing what is necessary.

Because the perception of value changes over time, the job of continuous improvement is never done. Kaizen must be repeated frequently using data and facts from relevant sources to guide improvement activities. Doing so will ensure that the university and its academic programs remain competitive, and also reflect deeper individual and institutional commitment to quality and continuous improvement.

Kaizen can also be used as a rational, fact-based, and non-zero-sum basis to combine or eliminate courses and degree programs whose relevancy has waned. Most universities offer many more courses and programs than they can effectively deliver. The faculty who created these courses and programs had very good intentions, but circumstances change over time, and so there is a periodic need for cleaning. The kaizen process can do this in ways that do not harm students or faculty.

Kaizen is not committee work. But, kaizen can be used to improve committee work; to improve workflows within and between process steps, and connect committee processes. Kaizen can also be used to improve the structure and work of university committees. For example, it is common to find more than 30 different committees in a university such as:

- Academic Assessment
- Academic Integrity
- Academic Standards

- Academic Advising
- Animal Care and Use
- Athletic Board
- Budget
- Curriculum
- Disabilities
- Distinguished Service
- Diversity
- Environmental Sustainability
- Excellence in Teaching
- Excellence in Research
- Facilities Planning
- Faculty Senate
- Foundation Grants
- Graduate Studies
- Human Studies
- Information Technology
- International Studies
- Library
- Mediation
- Parking and Traffic Appeals
- Promotion and Tenure
- Sabbatical Leave
- Safety
- Scholarship
- Student Affairs
- Student Appeals
- Substance Abuse
- Termination
- Trustees Awards
- University Professorships
- Women and Minorities

The Lean thinker would ask: "Is shared governance necessary for everything, or for some things?" Were Morris Cooke alive today, he would probably suggest that faculty share governance in Curriculum, Graduate Studies, and Promotion and Tenure committees, for example, and forego much of the rest. Cooke would want the faculty to spend their freed-up committee time on improving courses and teaching, and spending more time with students (not on research). He would be happy to see faculty participate in kaizen – both in administrative and academic processes – and have it count as their service contribution. Faculty might like that as well.

The reality is that many committees meet infrequently, while others are central to the university's purpose such as Curriculum. So the questions are: Which committees can be combined, which can be eliminated? Which require faculty, and which do not? What about academic departments' does it make sense to combine some? Will eliminating categorical distinctions within schools (e.g. accounting, marketing, operations management, etc., departments) help faculty work more closely together? What about academic advising; how can that be improved? And so on.

Question everything; that is what Lean people do. They think, ask questions, and improve.

Kaizen is not an evil thing. It is simply a process for improvement that requires outcomes to be non-zero-sum in order to be considered improvements. It is a process that greatly helps eliminate decision-making traps and illogical thinking. It is a process for learning, for improving information flow, and creates an organizational culture that asks "Why?" Kaizen promotes human creativity and innovation, helps lower costs, and reduces barriers for interacting with others. Kaizen improves people's understanding of the work, makes managers smarter, and helps to identify future leaders. Kaizen changes people's beliefs, it is fun, and it makes work more fulfilling. But you have to do it right to get the benefits.

To gain a much better understanding of kaizen, please read this important book:

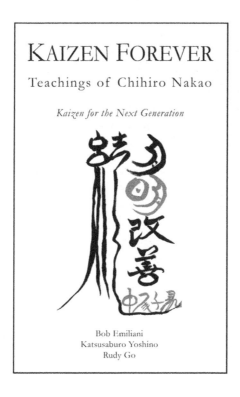

KAIZEN FOREVER

Teachings of Chihiro Nakao

Kaizen for the Next Generation

Bob Emiliani
Katsusaburo Yoshino
Rudy Go

Notes

[1] I. Kato and A. Smalley, *Toyota Kaizen Methods*, CRC Press, Boca Raton, FL, 2011

[2] M. Imai, *Gemba Kaizen*, McGraw-Hill, New York, NY, 1997

[3] M.L. Emiliani, "Using Kaizen to Improve Graduate Business School Degree Programs," *Quality Assurance in Education*, Vol. 13, No. 1, 2005, pp. 37-52

[4] M.L. Emiliani, "Team Leader's Kaizen Manual For Academic Courses and Programs," unpublished work, 2002 (updated 2009, 2012, and 2013).

7

Leadership Roles and Responsibilities

Lean management requires leaders to be open-minded, to question accepted wisdom, and to continuously improve their problem-solving skills. This means actually doing formal root cause analysis to find the true causes of problems and identify practical countermeasures.

For example, university presidents and others are concerned about undergraduate graduation rates. This is an important concern for which administrators receive great pressure. But is the problem encumbered by illogical thinking and decision-making traps that lead to expensive or ineffective solutions?

To improve graduation rates, universities create first year experience courses, retention plans, advising centers, tutoring centers, mentoring programs, and so on. Do these really address the problem? Or, are they focused on the symptoms? These are expensive solutions. Money was spent instead of ideas.

Universities must also contend with legislative mandates to academic programs, a political environment well known to suffer from inferior problem-solving skills (e.g. no root cause analysis). Their solutions almost always address symptoms, typically with little or no involvement or input of the key stakeholders who must implement the legislation. This bad process will surely result in major errors, despite well-intentioned efforts to improve graduation rates. The errors will lead to costly and time-consuming re-work, and cause immense frustration among faculty.

To avoid mandated outcomes, Lean leaders are exceptional and persistent problem solvers. They use structured problem-solving processes to illuminate root causes of problems [1]. This enables the identification, evaluation, and implementation of low-cost practical countermeasures.

Amazingly, improving teaching is rarely, if ever, part of the solution to the graduation rate problem. That is because university leaders' thinking is influenced by two assumptions:

- Teaching is generally excellent.
- Teaching plays no role in the graduation rate problem.

These are false assumptions that prevent desperately needed improvements in teaching. University leaders who spend the bulk of their time outside the classroom do not know the details pertaining to the value creating part of university work: teaching. Thus, they are beholden to false assumptions. Lean leaders know what is going on. They have an exceptionally clear view of the details involved in value-creating activities that are central to the organization's purpose.

Most improvements in teaching can be obtained at no cost. Other teaching improvements can be obtained at low cost. It is irresponsible of leadership not to pursue such opportunities.

University leaderships' failure to use structured problem-solving processes means that people's perception of problems will usually be vague or incorrect, and their solutions will usually be expensive and off target. People almost always spend money to solve problems. The normal things that universities do to improve graduation rates may indeed be helpful. But one thing is for certain: Important causes are left unaddressed when the problem-solving is ad hoc.

Think of the fishbone (cause-effect) diagram used in root cause analysis. Visually, it tells leaders that an effect lies in five or six cause categories, of which there are dozens of secondary, tertiary, quaternary, etc., causes that contribute to the observed effect. Low graduation rates are driven by multiple causes, some of which may be improved by first year experience courses, retention plans, advising centers, tutoring centers, mentoring programs, and the like. It is inescapable that teaching is a significant cause for the observed effect. But let's say that teaching plays zero role in graduation rates; that there is no causal relationship to the observed effect. Does that mean teaching should not be improved? Of course not, because ineffective teaching will be a big driver of other important problems.

Thus, a primary leadership role in Lean management is to be good at structured problem-solving and be a highly capable evaluator of the problem-solving. This means embracing the responsibility to know problem-solving well enough to teach others so that they can autonomously recognize problems, know how to quickly analyze them, and identify and implement practical countermeasures.

Lean management in a university will need to be supported by trustees, or, in the case of public universities, departments of higher education, legislators, and governors. University leadership will have to do the work of gaining their support because the President-trustee (or governor) interface will be affected. In addition, Lean management will affect budgets and people, principally though re-allocation of existing resources.

Leaders' roles and responsibilities in Lean management change in other ways that reflect the focus on structured problem-solving and the elimination of waste, unevenness, and unreasonableness. Humility is the attribute that unlocks the door. You cannot be a Lean leader if you think or act like you know it all or have all the answers. You have to be comfortable not knowing, and exploring new territory with others as a regular member of the team.

People in high positions often think they know things that they do not. Knowing is seen as a substitute for having done something. Leaders cannot know about Lean management without doing it. Therefore, academic administrators and non-academic managers must participate in kaizen and apply Lean thinking to their jobs. To be seen as credible by university personnel, leaders must do as they ask others to do. There is no way around that.

As you begin your Lean journey, your schedule of daily activities must change to help you develop new ways of thinking. Along the way, you will begin to ask questions about the work that you do. The kinds of questions that presidents, provost, senior managers, deans, supervisors, and department chairs will ask include:

- Do I really need to approve this? Can someone at lower levels do that?
- Is this meeting really necessary?
- Do these committees need this many members?
- What is our decision-making process?
- How can we improve it? How can we reduce they cycle time from data and facts to decision?
- How can we improve information flow?
- Can we reduce the number of reports generated by 50 percent?
- Can we shorten all reports by 90 percent and standardize report formats?
- Can we make the information we need visual and at-a-glance?
- What can we do to set university personnel up to succeed?
- What person or team should make this decision?
- How can we improve our visibility and accessibility to university personnel?
- What needs to change so I can spend some time every month participating in process improvement?
- Are we using too many metrics? Are they relevant? Are they too complex?
- Are the metrics we use consistent with Lean principles and practices? Or, do they generate waste, unevenness, and unreasonableness?
- Can we reduce the number of job classifications?
- Does our faculty hiring process support flexibility in human resource management?
- Are we working on too many things? What are the vital few things that the university must do?
- What leadership processes are we engaged in? How can they be improved?

- Can we standardize our leadership processes to improve leadership quality, reliability, and effectiveness?
- What do we need to do to get "instant information" to help us manage?
- What are our untested beliefs and assumptions?
- What decision-making traps do we regularly fall into?
- Which forms of illogical thinking are we most susceptible to?
- Can we begin to make conscious efforts to reduce organizational politics? Let's try to get rid of it so it does not obscure reality or slow down decision-making.
- What are we doing that we should not be doing?
- Can we improve our budgeting process from 9 months to 6 months to 3 months to 1 month to 2 weeks?
- Is our strategic plan practical? Or, is it filled with crap designed to satisfy our egos and dazzle our superiors – but unlikely to actually get done?
- Can we simplify our strategy and goals so they fit on one page [3]?
- Can our strategy be simple, such as "Teach well"?
- How do we get the trustees (or DHE, legislators, or governor) personally involved in Lean?

Can you think of other questions to ask that challenge the status quo?

Lean leaders must serve as role models, instill curiosity in others, allow people to think, give timely feedback often, praise people for their improvements and for following the processes, help people maintain focus on eliminating queues and getting information to flow, and help make Lean fun. People are drawn to fun activities. If you make Lean a burden, and it will quickly disappear.

Lean leaders must also help people overcome their barriers. Two barriers that you will run into among faculty and staff are, 1) the perception that Lean management is for repetitive work, such as manufacturing. And, 2) it applies to administration and not to academic work. Teachers will say their work is non-repetitive, as if their creative work is much like that of visual artists. The fact is, most of the work activities done by visual artists are repetitive, with a small portion of it non-repetitive. Likewise, most of what teachers do is repetitive, with some small portion of work being non-repetitive.

Another barrier is that people will think standardized work means that once the work is improved it does not change. That is incorrect. Standardized work is updated often as team members think of new ways to improve. Standardized work is subject to continuous improvement and therefore is not static. Or, people will say that their work cannot be standardized. Their challenge is to figure out which parts of the work can be standardized, and which cannot – and why not – to reduce errors and re-work and improve process quality and reliability. Doing so is in everyone's interest. You can help overcome this barrier by using standardized work for your own leadership processes [4].

University leaders should have in their work areas visual displays of information that inform people of the status of important processes at a glance. Such visual process management should be ubiquitous throughout the university. Improvement ideas should be managed visually as well, not hidden in computer systems. There should be places for people to write down ideas as they think of them and for their team to evaluate on a weekly basis (in a non-blaming, non-judgmental way). University leaders should look for and regularly evaluate visual management as they walk around campus.

University leaders should also spend as little time in their offices as possible and as much time as they can with university personnel and other stakeholders. They should also devise a simple and fair plan to share any actual cost savings (not cost avoidance) with employees, distributed on a quarterly basis. Doing so provides additional incentive to engage in daily improvement.

This chapter has given you a sense of leadership roles and responsibilities as they pertain to Lean management. There is more to know. You will learn by doing. Do not fool yourself into thinking that your knowledge of conventional management in any way informs you of Lean management. In fact, viewing the two as equivalent will assure failure.

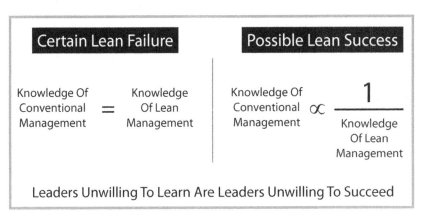

And, to get good at anything, including Lean management, leaders have to apply Lean principles and practices every day.

Notes

[1] J. Liker, *The Toyota Way*, McGraw-Hill, New York, NY, 2004. See p. 256 for a diagram of Toyota's practical problem-solving process.

[2] J. Shook, *Managing to Learn: Using the A3 Management Process*, Lean Enterprise Institute, Cambridge, MA, 2008

[3] B. Emiliani et al., *Better Thinking, Better Results*, The CLBM, LLC, Wethersfield, Conn., second edition, 2007, pp. 24-33

[4] M.L. Emiliani, "Standardized Work for Executive Leadership," *Leadership and Organizational Development Journal*, Vol. 29, No. 1, 2008, pp. 24-46

8

Beginner's Errors to Avoid

Let's discuss three grand mistakes that leaders make: viewing Lean narrowly as cost-cutting; perpetuating organizational politics; and indiscriminate use of Lean consultants. Following that is a list of 25 common errors that range in magnitude from great to small. All are important; please familiarize yourself with each one.

Lean management is often misunderstood as a cost-cutting "program." This narrow financial perspective often emerges as a result of either sudden or long-standing cost (budget) problems. Invariably, the value-creating part of the organization (operations, or in this case its equivalent, academics) gets starved for resources (budget cuts, unfilled positions, layoffs, etc.). This makes it very difficult for the value-creators to do their jobs. Efforts to save the organization usually backfire. By fundamentally misunderstanding Lean management, more and bigger problems are created. This is the first grand mistake that leaders make.

The purpose of Lean management is to grow and improve – both people and the organization. The principles, methods, and tools are intended to develop human resources so that the value proposition for customers can be improved over time, and the organization and its stakeholders continue to prosper. If finance has a leading role at your university, its role changes to that of a supporting role in Lean management. The value-creating unit (academics) takes the leading role because it is a principal source of cash generation and customer satisfaction. Academics, the raison d'être of a university, is never starved for resources, nor is it given anything that it asks for. In Lean, people use ideas and creativity to solve problems. Sometimes additional resources are needed. Management simply asks that teams thoroughly investigate no-cost and low-cost alternatives. Resources will be provided if they are actually needed. Lean management, done right, will reverse the decades-long trend of starving academic units of resources.

Lean management never asks something for nothing. In contrast, it is common in conventional management for leaders to ask for something and provide no money, material, equipment, space, energy, people, time, etc. This is illogical, and so people spend their time talking about how stupid management's request is. This must never happen in Lean. People need resources to do things, even if they are small. People will need time, space, and a small budget to do kaizen.

Because teaching is labor intensive, it is easy for university leaders to think that their budget problems are due to high labor costs. What Lean management teaches people to do is closely monitor all costs and work continuously to reduce costs, but not by cutting heads. High labor costs are due to cumbersome processes that require many more people to operate than are actually necessary. Management owns the process problem, and employees must not be the ones to pay.

Employees whose work is no longer required as a result of process improvement must be re-deployed elsewhere in the organization. They will help other areas that are overloaded with work or work on kaizen teams until a position becomes available or until they can be trained to do a different job. This will be done as a mutual-gains negotiation to assure good outcomes. No employee will be unemployed as a result of kaizen.

Politics is a major distraction that greatly impairs an organization's ability to respond to customers and to changes in the marketplace, for example. Leaders must begin to see organizational politics as waste and as something that can be substantially reduced – if not largely eliminated – to help employees align around a common objective: continuous improvement.

Organizational politics must be seen for what it actually is: an activity that adds cost but creates no value. It causes enormous delays in decision-making, mistakes, and re-work. It frustrates people who want to do good things and it wastes their lives.

Adopting Lean management yet continuing long-standing political routines is the second grand mistake that leaders make.

Inconsistencies such as this must be eliminated to the greatest extent possible. Employees will find many policies, practices, metrics, and so on to be inconsistent with Lean management. You must not dismiss them. These policies, practices, metrics will need to be made consistent, one-by-one, or eliminated. This is good work for kaizen teams to do.

The third grand mistake that leaders make involves the use of Lean consultants. Leaders often think it wise to obtain the support of consultants to help initiate and accelerate new ways of doing things. This may be appropriate, and there are some very good Lean consultants to choose from [1]. However, university leaders must recognize the serious potential pitfalls associated with using Lean consultants.

Consultants are skilled at telling decision-makers exactly what they want to hear. They skillfully ensnare top leaders in decision-making traps (anchoring, framing, confirmation bias, estimating and forecasting). They will sell you hard on their ability to capably deploy Lean in your university and deliver fast, measurable results. You should be very skeptical. It is as if someone said they could teach you to play guitar like Eric Clapton in a year or two. It is not going to happen.

What nearly every consultant is selling you is zero-sum half-Lean: "Continuous Improvement" without the "Respect for People." The history of doing his stretches back over 100 years and is well documented [2]. Consultant led zero-sum half-Lean causes enormous employee dissatisfaction and organizational unrest, and little actual improvement is achieved. Employees are repelled by half-Lean and want nothing to do with it [3]. Management has a choice: abandon Lean or try for a do-over. Good luck either way.

If you decide to use a consultant, use the university's normal Request for Proposal (RFP) process (cumbersome as it may currently be). Do not pick a consultant based on your golf partner's recommendation. Carefully identify your needs in the RFP. Ask how the consultant comprehends and deploys the "Respect for People" principle. If it is limited to one 30-slide PowerPoint training module out of many others that are focused on Lean tools, then they can be eliminated from consideration.

Ask the consultant how they comprehend Lean leadership and what Lean management asks of the organization's leaders. If what they say is "support" from leaders and not much more, then you can eliminate those consultants from consideration. You want your RFP to cite the Lean management system, and eliminate all responses that focus principally on learning and using Lean tools. This formulation of Lean management is more than three decades old and does not represent current thinking.

Most Lean consultants are expensive, yet it is a buyers' market for Lean consulting services. So, ask for a lot and get a good price. Be aware that most top-tier consultants (the consulting generalists) do not understand Lean management. They understand Lean tools and will implement them in your university to achieve short-term cost savings. Remember, most consultants equate improved performance with job cuts. Your university will be subject to their creative destruction.

Non-profits often look for cheap alternatives to save money. They sometimes call on area businesses experienced in Lean to offer free Lean training. Be careful. In most cases, for-profit businesses understand Lean narrowly and incorrectly as cost-cutting and layoffs to improve productivity. University employees will think the same thing will happen to them as what happened to their private-sector counterparts if you use trainers from area businesses.

Pro-bono private sector services for Lean training signals to employees and others that Lean is not really that important. People quickly recognize that what gets resourced is important, and what does not get resourced isn't important. They will view Lean as nice to do, and a few good things will surely happen, but it will not be seen by employees as a must-do. That will result in varying levels of buy-in and teamwork, which normally slows down the rate of improvement and sets the stage for isolated improvement. Universities need broad-based improvement.

University leaders would be wise to study the non-profit healthcare approach to Lean transformation. It has been effective in some cases at engaging senior administrators in daily Lean practice and the targeted use of Lean consultants [4].

Another alternative model university leaders can consider is do-it-yourself Lean. There are many low cost resources (books, journal papers, training, etc.), that university personnel can learn from and put into practice. In addition, university leaders can harness enthusiasm for change by appointing current employees to new roles as internal Lean consultants. Seek volunteers among faculty, staff, and administration who want to focus their work on leading improvement throughout the university. Doing this shows confidence in university employees – that they are capable people who can learn new things and teach others – unlike the message that is typically sent to employees when consultants are hired: You have failed and you are incapable of making things better. The best Lean practitioners either never used consultants or used them sparingly to achieve specific objectives.

Here are 25 more beginner's errors to avoid:

1. Characterizing Lean management as an "initiative," a "program," or a "regimen" gives people the impression that Lean is an activity that will soon pass.

2. Characterizing kaizen as an "event," "blitz," "project," "burst," or "project" carries connotations that do not accurately portray the meaning or intent of kaizen.

3. Thinking that your conception of teamwork is the same as teamwork in a Lean environment. In conventional management teamwork is often forced, political, and zero-sum

in its orientation. In a Lean environment teamwork is natural, harmonious, and non-zero-sum.

4. Mistaking a little Lean knowledge for a lot of Lean knowledge. You cannot read the first 100 pages of a book and know Lean management.

5. Adding new Lean knowledge without eliminating old conventional management knowledge. New Lean knowledge must displace old knowledge and practices that are inconsistent with Lean.

6. Thinking you can become good at Lean management without having to practice every day. Proficiency in anything requires enduring commitment to daily practice.

7. Thinking the leadership skills that got you to where you are will work in a Lean environment. The beliefs, behaviors, and competencies of leaders skilled in the Lean management system are completely different than those possessed by managers skilled in conventional management practices.

8. Thinking that Lean management is theory. Lean was developed by practitioners who faced real-world problems; tangible opportunities or threats to their existence. Lean is grounded in the reality that zero-sum thinking leads to bad outcomes while non-zero-sum thinking leads to better outcomes.

9. Failing to recognize that the core competency concept is incompatible with Lean. Subscribing to the core competencies concept usually results in outsourcing work that is not important to managers, but is often very important to customers. Managers do not understand this because they lack a clear grasp of the customer's perception of value.

10. Adopting Lean but not changing performance measurement metrics. All metrics currently in use need to be critically examined. Do they create or perpetuate waste, unevenness, or

unreasonableness? If so, then eliminate them or de-emphasize their significance or use.

11. Remaining fixated on labor costs and unit costs, and not understanding total costs.

12. Not establishing a no-blame policy. Making a no-blame policy come to life every day is the responsibility of all university leaders.

13. Not establishing a "no layoffs due to kaizen" policy. University leaders have to make it safe for people to improve. If they do not do this, then people will not participate in kaizen.

14. Continuing to make decisions "by the numbers" and failing to incorporate non-quantitative information. Lean leaders always include non-quantitative information in decision-making. They know that just because you cannot put something into a financial spreadsheet doesn't mean it is not real.

15. Continuing inability to comprehend cause-and-effect; e.g. squeezing suppliers to obtain lower unit prices on purchased goods and services and thinking they will not find a way to get even and charge a higher price when the opportunity to do so arises.

16. Thinking Lean management can work in a political workplace. Lean management thrives on merit and withers on wasteful organizational politics. Politics and politically-based decisions contradicts Lean management. Leaders must be committed to logic, knowledge, detail, facts, and reality.

17. Mandating levels of Lean accomplishment by certain points in time. Doing this politicizes Lean and turns it into a superficial game.

18. Making Lean complex. People have a tendency to make simple things complex (e.g. testing and assessment). Lean made complex is a recipe for failure. Keep it simple. Stick to the fundamentals and practice every day.

19. Confusing internal policies that can be changed with externally mandated requirements that cannot (or will take time to influence change). Internal policies should be carefully examined to see if they are truly needed or can be improved to be less onerous. You will find many internal policies do not directly address the root causes of problems.

20. Thinking you know what the "Respect for People" principle means. It takes years of thought and practice to comprehend what the "Respect for People" principle means, and how this principle relates to the "Continuous Improvement" principle. Leaders must also understand how the "Respect for People" principle relates to the university's strategic plan, goals, metrics, and key stakeholders.

21. Thinking that Lean will one day stick. It is wrong for administrators to think that if people practice Lean for several years, it will eventually stick; that it will become part of the university's DNA. Lean requires constant attention, maintenance, and improvement to keep it alive and healthy. People keep Lean alive through the daily application of Lean principles and practices.

22. Not planning for changes in leadership. Lean dies when the top leaders who were interested in Lean leave the university and are replaced with leaders who have no interest in Lean management.

23. Cherry-picking the Lean management system to achieve short-term gains. For over 100 years, managers have cherry-picked select concepts, methods, and tools to obtain short-term gains, thus guaranteeing poor results or failure.

24. Using Lean tools to fine-tune the status quo. Tweaking the current state in response to competitive pressures is not leadership; it is laziness. Seeking to fine-tune assumes that the university is near its optimum, which is surely not the case.

25. Hiding from employees. Lean leaders do not stay in the office and isolate themselves from employees (or students or other stakeholders). They instead engage employees and "go see" to understand what is really going on.

In the old days, managers who adopted Lean had to figure these things out for themselves. As a result, they stumbled along and often made slow progress. There is no need for you to repeat their mistakes. You can avoid these beginner's errors by using resources that are widely available such as this and other books, by speaking to Lean leaders, attending Lean conferences, and so on.

Follow this Lean transformation model and you will do quite well.

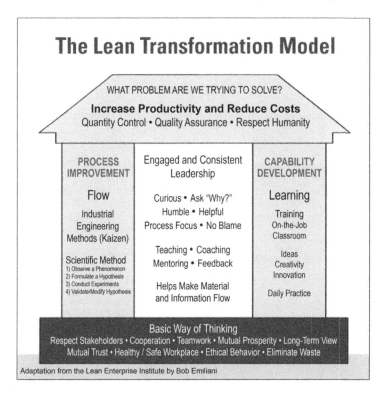

Notes

[1] The author (B.E.) is a teacher, researcher, and author. He is not a consultant. At the time of publication of this book, the author has no business relationship with any consultant.

[2] B. Emiliani, *REAL LEAN: Critical Issues and Opportunities in Lean Management*, Volume Two, The CLBM, LLC, Wethersfield, Conn., 2007, Chapters 1-6, 10, and 11.

[3] See the cock-up that occurred at Her Majesty's Revenue and Customs (U.K.) when managers selected Lean consultant narrowly focused on continuous improvement tools and rapid deployment thereof. B. Carter *et al.*, "Lean and Mean in the Civil Service: The Case of Processing in HMRC," *Public Money & Management*, Vol. 31, Issue 2, 2011, pp. 115-122. Read my commentary on Carter's paper: B. Emiliani, "Lean Management Failure at HMRC," *Management Services*, The Journal of the Institute of Management Services, Vol. 55, No. 4, Winter 2011, pp. 13-15

[4] C. Kenney, *Transforming Healthcare*, CRC Press, Boca Raton, FL, 2011.

9

Expected Outcomes

The expected outcome is for the "students matter most" rhetoric to match reality as closely as possible. Students should see steady improvement in the quality of teaching and of courses and degree programs. Educational experiences will be marked with a tangible sense of value that others cannot easily replicate. Your university will be distinctive and students will celebrate their decision to attend. For this to happen, academics must take center-stage in academic institutions, and it will shine more brightly than it ever has. Administrative processes that support academics will shine as well.

The journey will not be easy, but it will be a lot of fun if you do it right and people will take great pride in their work. Leaders must lead, and administrators, faculty, and staff must learn the thinking, skills, and capabilities needed to support daily Lean practice. They will engage in daily problem-solving using Lean principles and practices, not for just for the big problems, but for the small problems as well. This means that everyone will start thinking in ways they may have not thought before, and doing things they have never done before. The "Respect for People" principle will never be downgraded or dismissed. Doing so is the fast track to failure.

Faculty will ask questions that most will have never asked themselves before, such as:

- Is this activity value-added, non-value-added but necessary, or is it waste?
- How can we eliminate waste, unevenness, and unreasonableness?
- How can we improve information flow?

University employees, including top leaders, will ask these same
questions for the work that they do.

Faculty, specifically, will ask questions such as:

- Can the faculty in my department do a better job of sharing
  our improvement ideas and successes?
- I like it when my courses are "in the can" (i.e. "done").
  Isn't that inconsistent with the "Continuous Improvement"
  and "Respect for People" principles? Maybe I should
  update my courses more often to keep up with the times.
- How can I improve my lectures? Can I make them more
  participative? Can I relate them to everyday things that
  students recognize to help them understand the material
  better?
- Am I wasting students' time by asking them to do that
  assignment? Do they get anything out of it?
- Why do students queue-up outside my office every
  semester? Is that necessary?
- How can I make assignments and test questions less
  ambiguous?
- Can I mistake-proof assignment instructions?
- Should I create a checklist to make sure I am prepared for
  class?
- Should I give the students a standard format for
  completing assignments? Might that improve the accuracy
  and speed of grading?
- Are term papers really necessary for my course? How else
  can students develop writing and thinking skills?
- How can I make this material more interesting and
  engaging?
- If I did not use up class time giving tests, what other things
  could I teach students during that time. What activity could
  students do during that time?
- How can I better distribute the workload of the course and
  the assignments over the semester?

- How can I level-load grading; do a little grading every day rather than big batches all at once?
- How can I improve the relevancy of my course to the real world (lecture, reading, and assignments)?
- How can I impart more tacit knowledge to students? What unique insights can I offer based on my experiences?
- Should I record my lectures and use class time to share tacit knowledge and facilitate problem-solving?
- Do I really need to use a $200 textbook in every course I teach? Are textbooks even necessary for my courses?
- Can I incorporate the Caux Round Table *Principles for Responsible Business* in any of my courses?
- Can I incorporate formal root cause analysis in my courses (5 Whys and fishbone diagrams) to greatly improve students' critical thinking skills? What about PDCA or A3 reports?
- Is the way I teach consistent with the "Continuous Improvement" and "Respect for People" principles?

If faculty asks these questions, and more, then they will begin to receive student feedback such as:

"This is the first course I've had where I can focus on learning."

"Test taking tends to encourage a narrow focus of studying to retain information for the purposes of a test. There is little retention or fundamental understanding of the concepts you try to memorize for an exam, or the connection between the material and application may be missed. This class is structured in a way that the reading and homework develop the fundamentals of what the course is trying to teach. The open class discussions on the readings brings out a further understanding of the material and where/how you can use it."

"Did you know, from all the classes I have taken, yours have been the one that impacted me the most!"

"I really enjoyed this class – it is one that I can assure you will be remembered and referenced in coming years."

Application of Lean management in a university should result in other important outcomes. It can provide a sensible and respectful pathway for less skilled teachers to focus more on research, and vice versa. And it should result in a more dynamic relationship between teaching, research, and improvement (service).

It should result in standardized syllabi and lecture notes for first and second year courses. There should be division of labor so that faculty can focus on teaching and research, with "trivial activities" (Cooke's words) transferred to administrative aides (of which you will probably need to hire more). Faculty should be cross-trained to teach different courses, and create a practical mentoring process for senior faculty to coach junior faculty.

It should result in budget for improving teaching, speaking, presentation, and discussion facilitating skills, or establish alternate ways for faculty to contribute to teaching. Lean management gives administrators the chance to prove they are serious about good teaching [1].

It should result in changes to the hiring process to give equal opportunities to academically qualified people from industry, to increase diversity among faculty and to enhance students' educational experiences. It should result in the hiring of multi-skilled faculty capable of teaching different disciplines such as math and engineering or science and business. It should result in greater flexibility and adaptability to changing circumstances.

The expected outcomes should be remarkable. If it is not, then you need to improve your understanding and practice of Lean management. There will be many problems along the way to delivering better education to students, while assuring academic rigor and appropriate learning outcomes.

A curious, humble, persistent, and enthusiastic university president eager to learn and do new things can expect Lean management to help do the kinds of things they have probably long wanted to do. And there will be a lot of fun along the way.

Notes

[1] Pop quiz! Presidents, what do you think a Lean person would think about NCAA athletic programs in colleges and universities? What do you think a Lean person would think about intramural athletic programs?

10

Closing Remarks

I wrote this book for one simple reason: to introduce to university leaders a better way to develop people and to improve processes in higher education. If you have made it this far, then you must be truly interested in Lean management. Congratulations. This puts you in the company of select others who are far along in their careers yet enjoy learning and experiencing new things.

More than 100 years ago, Frederick Winslow Taylor said that Scientific Management requires a "mental revolution" by both managers and workers. I think it is more accurate to say that Lean management requires a mental evolution by managers and workers. Administrators, faculty, and staff who have long practiced or been subjected to conventional management should grow weary of its demands, the problems that it generates, and outcomes that often fall well below expectations. Evolution in management thinking and practice begins when people become tired and ready for change. Are you tired enough to evolve?

If not, then the only way to meet current and future challenges in higher education is by using the same old zero-sum routines to solve problems: perpetual budget cutting, reorganization, and so on. If that is what you choose, then I have failed in this book to convince you of the merits of Lean management. As we part ways, I want you to know that I wish you and all university stakeholders the very best.

For those few university leaders that wish to proceed, you can look forward to a fun new experience that will be very challenging yet more rewarding than anything you have ever experienced in higher education. Lean management gives you the opportunity to align the rhetoric of teaching excellence, learning, affordability, value, student engagement and so on, with reality. You have also chosen a path that allows you to better control your destiny and leave mandated academic requirements for other universities to contend with. With Lean, you will witness the greatness of human potential, rather than people simply doing what they are told – or only what "the system" allows them to do. I am optimistic that faculty, in particular, are more adaptable than most realize, and that they will do far better than is thought possible.

Your immediate goal should be to develop a simple plan consistent with Lean thinking that aligns leadership at all levels and prepares everyone for what is to come. This will not be easy, and you will hear thousands of complains. You must address these, one-by-one, in a manner that is consistent with the "Respect for People" principle. This will be your first big test.

Within a few years, you should see significant improvements in academic courses and programs, and a narrowing of the gap between cost and value. Concurrently, processes will be improved and allow the university to reduce the magnitude of price increases or eliminate them all together in the future. There should also be opportunities to reduce tuition and fees over time, allowing students and payers to see greater value in their higher education experience than its cost. However, they will see this only if administrators, faculty, and staff can accept the reality that continuous improvement never ends.

If all goes well, faculty will understand Lean management as a non-threatening way to help people improve the work they do, one that has always focused far more on effectiveness than on mechanistic efficiency. They will be satisfied that teaching, academic rigor, and student learning continuously improve, and that they are integral parts of the processes that help make that happen.

In closing, I want university leaders to clearly understand two things: First, leaders have as much to lean as they do to unlearn. Fortunately, these two processes occur concurrently with active participation in continuous improvement activities. You will need some Lean training and read some good books. Let this one be your guide.

Second, as smart you may be, it is critical that you never assume greater understanding of the "Respect for People" than is actually the case. This understanding crosses a wide range of activities and circumstances, many of which are learned only through personal experience. People will not participate in daily improvement if they sense zero-sum outcomes. They will instead be quickly repelled.

Finally, managers always ask: "How do we get a Lean culture?" Answer: Everyone in the university, top to bottom, applies Lean principles and practices daily, in some way. It is much like learning to play piano, where a little practice every day builds the necessary skills and capabilities [1, 2]. But, unlike music practice that is for a couple of hours per day, Lean thinking and practice are applied to work throughout the day.

And, please remember:

"It ceases to be Lean management the
moment it is used for bad."

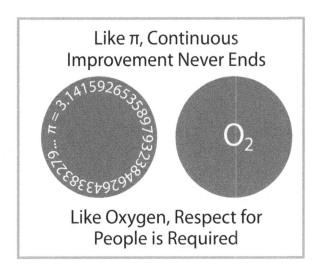

Notes

[1] M.L. Emiliani and M. Emiliani, "Music as a Framework to Better Understand Lean Leadership," forthcoming in *Leadership and Organizational Development Journal*, Volume 34, Issue 5, 2013. This paper presents an innovative and creative way to explain why senior managers typically have great difficulty comprehending and correctly practicing Lean leadership. It describes the depth and richness of relationships between Lean management and music. It will help leaders improve their understanding of Lean management, how to learn it, and how to lead a Lean transformation.

[2] See also *Lean IS Healthcare*, by B. Emiliani, The CLBM, LLC, Wethersfield, Conn., 2012

Afterword

Continuous Flow University

My book *Lean University* presented a practical pathway for significantly improving traditional classroom- and hybrid-based education in ways that students and payers will recognize as being highly beneficial. There is no doubt that they will say, "This is great! Why did it take you so long to do this?" Given the high value associated with daily personal contact between students and teachers, students with other students, and faculty with other faculty, staff, and administrators, it is imperative that such improvements are made quickly. Overall, the traditional model of classroom-based higher education has been effective at achieving desired outcomes and will continue to exist far into the future.

Yet, other improvements must be made in parallel to take advantage of information technologies that have become integral parts of students' lives and daily learning experiences. Faculty and administrators must recognize these technological changes and respond to them quickly and intelligently, as a large segment of students will view web-based delivery as their preferred means to take courses.

In addition, managers throughout modern history have eagerly adopted new technologies for the various promises that they offer, imperfect though they may be while in their infancies. It is true that the businesses that offer new technologies often oversell and under-deliver. However, in most cases they work tirelessly to overcome the limitations that traditionalists identify as the core reasons why the new technology will not be effective. Current fears regarding the depersonalization of higher education, loss of community, and decline in educational effectiveness may soon be recognized as overblown.

With this in mind, I present a vision of a university that strives to achieve even greater flow than previously outlined – in academic processes, in administrative and student support processes, and in students' education – aided by the use of technology. I call it "Continuous Flow University." This model allows students to "pull" educational services on-demand, in contrast to traditional delivery in higher education that is a "push" system. The *raison d'être* for creating Continuous Flow University is to serve a segment of students and payers far better than they have been served in the recent past. It is not to lower costs [1], or to compromise quality or educational effectiveness. Lower costs, wherever they are achieved, will be a byproduct of improved processes and improved pedagogies.

To make this vision a reality requires enterprise-wide adoption of Lean management and the rapid addition of web-based delivery of educational services to students – while simultaneously improving course content, teaching effectiveness, and academic rigor. This will include targeted development and judicious use of information technologies that exist now or in the near future.

There are many compelling reasons to better serve students and payers, including the need to improve productivity and increase national and international competitiveness. In addition, administrators have let costs get out of control over the last 30 years and have been remarkably inattentive to quality [2]. These fundamental problems compromise the ability of any service organization to meet the needs of its customers and to survive long-term.

Two things in particular are worth noting: The first is recurring failures by leaders (and followers) of private corporations, public institutions, and of Wall Street (recent examples include Johnson & Johnson, Penn State, Barclays *et al.*). Executives who received top grades from top professors in top colleges and universities led nearly all such failures. This indicates that the way we educate our future leaders can be improved. While every professor says they teach critical thinking, observation of real-world outcomes proves otherwise. The quality of higher education is lower than we will admit, and more can be done to professionalize teaching.

Second is the recognition that higher education costs too much in relation to its quality and outcomes (not only with respect to major failures, education often goes unused by organizations whose internal culture is financially driven or highly political). Higher education delivers its services to students using the batch-and-queue method, which is always far more resource intensive than flow, because it consumes more money, space, time, material, people, equipment, energy, etc.

Will going from batch to flow actually make sense for higher education services? Will it result in better and less expensive services? Will it reduce the average time needed to obtain a degree? To answer these questions, let's look at higher education from the student's perspective. Along the way, let's also highlight some realities that students must contend with. If higher education can accept these current and emerging realities, then they would dramatically change the way they deliver their services to many students because it is better for *them*.

Let's begin with the prices that students and payers must contend with for higher education. Post-secondary education has outpaced the rate of inflation over the last 30 years, due principally to large increases in administrative processes and infrastructure expenses (and related debt service). During the same period, real wages for workers has stagnated or declined, while average household income has started to decline in recent years. In addition, starting salaries for new graduates has declined in many industries. So, there is an immediate need for substantial cost reduction – practically overnight. How do you do that?

When considering the total cost of higher education (tuition + all other expenses), two obvious expenses emerge: commuting costs for those students who do not live on campus, and living expenses for those who do live on campus. Reducing or eliminating the need for commuting to school would result in fuel, automobile (or bus, or train), parking, and time savings. This would yield single-digit percent savings for students, but which could be significant nonetheless. Eliminating on-campus living expenses (dorms, meal plans, etc.), would reduce students' total cost of higher education by about 50 percent.

Securing these savings for students requires colleges and universities to offer a second mode of delivery for degree programs, and reduce the need for students to obtain loans to finance their education. Students who demand the residential university social experience and classroom interaction, and who can afford it, will continue to pay more, while those who see less value in those experiences, or who cannot afford it, should pay less.

Everyone recognizes that companies, especially large employers, lay off employees at will, in good times and bad, for many different reasons (some are valid, most are nonsense). And, they complain incessantly in recent years about not being able to find people with the requisite skills. Employees affected by layoffs cannot wait to obtain new knowledge, skills, and diplomas according the traditional semester-based university schedule. There is simply too much time lost to waiting. And, it is too expensive to re-educate one's – potentially three or four times in a career.

In the future, workers will need to be more flexible in their mobility and go where the jobs are (for those jobs that require humans on-site). This means that education will have to follow the student as they move from location to location to maintain employment. Workers cannot be tied to the geographical location of campus classrooms. Education has to come to them, wherever they are, on a just-in-time basis. And, it has to be affordable – probably no more than $300 per 3-credit course ($12,000 for an undergraduate degree, and $3,000 for a 30-credit graduate degree [in 2015 dollars]). This price more accurately reflects the average student's available financial resources in the United States. Let's call this the actual market price; the price that students and families can pay without incurring substantial debt.

The pricing model normally used by universities assumes a non-competitive marketplace (sellers' market): price = cost + profit [3].

The equation universities must instead follow is (buyers' market): price - cost = profit. They must develop processes that are capable of delivering educational services at the actual market price, and then they must improve processes via kaizen to reduce costs and assure (or increase) profit. The equation, price - cost = profit, keeps university personnel focused on reducing costs, while the equation, price = cost + profit (classic "cost-plus"), keeps university personnel focused on growing enrollments (sales) – often irrespective of the university's capacity to serve students. The difference is being "university-focused" vs. being "student-focused."

Don't forget, cost reduction is far more powerful than price increases at contributing to profit. For a 20 percent gross margin business, one dollar in cost reduction is equivalent to increasing sales by 5 dollars. In addition, growing campus enrollments in the highly competitive market of higher education (among non-elite public and private institutions) is much more expensive than it is to reduce costs by improving processes. Increasing the marketing budget is easy to do, but it increases costs. Process improvement, however, is difficult, but it reduces costs and is far more needed.

Let's look at how the equation, price = cost + profit, leads to higher costs in the delivery of educational services (in addition to the many secondary and tertiary processes that are required as a result of long throughput times and process variation [4]). Take, for example, waiting. Nobody likes to wait, but waiting is pervasive in higher education. Waiting is bad because it adds cost and creates no value for students. Examples include:

- Waiting for admissions decisions
- Waiting to enroll in courses
- Waiting for the start of classes
- Waiting for interim and final grades
- Waiting for required courses to be offered
- Waiting for days between classes
- Waiting for teachers to respond to students

- Waiting for professors' office hours
- Waiting outside of professor's office
- Waiting for support services

These queues are also a great source of annoyance and frustration to students. They would be much happier if educational and administrative processes flowed with little or no interruption.

At Continuous Flow University, students would apply to the university online and receive same-day notification of acceptance or rejection (or, within 24 hours). Upon acceptance, students would not have to wait for their courses to start weeks or months later. They could begin the day they were accepted, the following day, or a week or two later – whatever best fits *their* schedule. If they need to take a break, they can do it any time they want and not have to wait for fall or spring break.

If a student can start a course any time, then that means courses must run continuously, 24 x 7 x 365. On any given day of the week, there could be 103 students on module 1, 48 students on module 3, 77 students on module 9, and 56 students on module 13. How can one professor manage such a situation? What if they are responsible for two or three online courses running continuously, where some students are degree seeking while others are not, and where students are dispersed globally with varying degrees of English speaking and writing skills? More on that later.

Students would take courses at their own pace. If they can absorb and process the material at three times the pace of a normal 3-credit hour semester-based course, then that is fine. They will have completed the course in four weeks instead of thirteen. If they absorb and process the material at one-third the pace of a normal semester-based course, then that is fine as well. The full- and part-time student time-limit for degree completion, whether face-to-face or online would likely remain the same, absent a bona fide learning disability.

Courses comprising online degrees may need to offer fewer, more focused electives, resulting in less customization to students' individual needs – yet there will be sufficient customization to satisfy most students' needs. A benefit would be the avoidance of costs and time associated with creating and offering numerous elective courses that are nice-to-have but otherwise non-essential. The development of new elective courses would continue, but in a far more focused way (and for face-to-face classes as well).

The various types of homework assignments commonly given to students would continue, but they will be leveled and tied to each module to avoid batching of information. Thirteen modules means there are thirteen homework assignments. Mid-term and final exams will not be necessary for most courses. Assignments will be evaluated automatically using software, with grades posted to students' accounts within minutes. This relieves professors of a time-consuming burden that strongly detracts from real-time continuous improvement of their courses and student interaction (and, to address the root causes of failures mentioned at the beginning of this Afterword).

Any person in the world could take a course anytime and complete the homework assignments for free. Their assignments will be graded by software, and feedback would be machine-generated. These students would receive no course credit. Instead, they would receive an acknowledgment for each course completed. They would not receive acknowledgement of completion of the courses required for a degree program, even if all such courses were completed.

To obtain a degree from the university, students would have to pay for the courses they take and would be assigned to a professor who provides human feedback. The professor would meet with hundreds of degree-seeking students at a time live or recorded via an online platform and provide tacit knowledge, observations, linkages between the course and current events, group feedback, etc. These would be scheduled as discrete events, two to three hours in duration, for all students that have completed 8 to 15 percent of the course, 35 to 50 percent of the course, and 70 to 100 percent of the course, for example.

Many academic programs and courses require extensive use of laboratory facilities (i.e. medicine, science, engineering). Over time, the learning that physical and mechanical experimentation and laboratory work confer to students will be conducted online using software simulations. Software development costs must be carefully controlled in order to affordably deliver the required features and avoid expensive and unnecessary add-ons [5]. These will be among the last courses and degree programs to be available completely online. However, degree programs that require high-touch, in-person interaction will likely remain largely in the traditional format – though effort should be made to improve flow for these courses and programs as well.

Software simulations of physical and mechanical experiments could have a downside – the lack of hands-on learning. It likely increase the gap between knowing and actual doing, and remain students' Achilles heel for which industry must continue to take responsibility for filling – provided they will actually hire graduates (vs. increasingly displace human resources with software and automation).

To eliminate the problem of repetitive questions coming from hundreds of online students, question-and-answer databases have to be created for each course over time. Once created, they should be continuously improved and also used by classroom-based students, thereby freeing professors from time-consuming tasks of having to answer the same questions over and over again, year after year.

So, what is the role of the professor? The professor will continue their work transforming information into knowledge and teaching that to students. Their course loads would be split between face-to-face classroom courses and online courses (for some the split would be 100%-zero, or vice versa). Professors would continue to do research, where required, but their service contribution would be substantially reduced and re-focused onto the curriculum. This will require professors to relinquish much of shared governance as it has been historically understood and practiced, and shift most non-curricular responsibilities to university administrators.

Professors would assume a role similar to product line managers. A designated team of professors would have specific responsibilities for the courses and degrees offered within a discipline, both face-to-face and online. The big difference is that more of their time would be spent collaboratively working on course design, content, and delivery to substantially improve both face-to-face and online courses. And, they would provide feed-forward guidance to students on common pitfalls to avoid, thereby helping to assure that the desired learning outcomes are achieved.

Importantly, professors will have to think much more critically about content and learning outcomes. In leading the kaizens at Rensselaer in 2002 [6, 7], I realized that most professors, working alone, are not nearly as good as they think they are when it comes to thinking critically about content and learning outcomes (myself included). They tend to put more material into courses than is actually required, and evaluations of students' work are typically too many and too complex. I have no doubt that kaizen applied to courses and to create a well-integrated curriculum will substantially improve the value proposition of both face-to-face and online courses. I also have no doubt that kaizen can help further professionalize teaching.

Relinquishing much of shared governance could cause problems. For example, administrators will have many more opportunities to behave in zero-sum ways: autocratic, bullying, and micromanaging. They will sometimes do things that could negatively affect curricular affairs, do things that are good for the university but bad for students, etc. This will quickly annoy key stakeholders (students, payers, faculty, and staff), the result of which will be to upset creativity, innovation, and teamwork, disrupt continuous flow, and initiate regression to batch-and-queue processing. This will, of course, reduce the quality and timeliness of educational services, and increase costs.

Various countermeasures are used in Lean management to avoid such outcomes, beginning with the "Respect for People" principle. Additional countermeasures include daily kaizen, visual controls, and assuring that those promoted into administrative leadership positions clearly understand their roles and responsibilities – which include helping to improve flow.

Cheating will be present in online courses just as it is in face-to-face courses. It can be mitigated by finger- and voice-print verification, and through certifications. Software will grade written text, while greater use could be made of oral exams, possibly recorded (also graded using software and posted to students' accounts within minutes). Colleges and universities will have to adopt plagiarism thresholds of 5 or 10 percent, to account for poor paraphrasing, subconscious plagiarism, etc., and to avoid needless and time-consuming disputes.

This essay described a vision for Continuous Flow University designed to better serve students in both academic and administrative and support processes, as well as the interests of payers and employers. It is in contrast to the pedestrian advice offered by top consultants for improving universities' financial condition. They proffer various schemes that yield temporary benefits, but most of which are difficult to manage effectively – though they generate big consulting fees. The cost for such advice is high, but the value is low because it is devoid of innovative thinking. And, the consultant's view of improvement is "university-focused" (price = cost + profit), not "student-focused" (price - cost = profit). They do not understand or talk about how flow is a lower cost and more effective way to serve students in academic, administration, and supporting services.

Instead, I am advocating a fun and inexpensive, mostly do-it-yourself, approach to improvement. Students will appreciate taking better courses that they can complete faster – likely 25 to 40 percent faster – if waiting is eliminated. There will be many challenges to manage through, including declining occupancy in dorms and classrooms, especially at second- and third-tier colleges and universities. Buildings will have to be re-purposed and some will be demolished and converted to open space.

If the leaders of colleges and universities pursue this vision carefully and intelligently, it might invite opportunities such as students becoming attached to your school for life-long educational services through paid subscriptions. Annuities are wonderful things to have. But, the value proposition for students must be compelling, and will likely have to include comprehensive life-long job placement services. After all, no job for the student means no annuity for the college or university.

We might also want to think differently about faculty pay. Meaning, how to increase pay for the value-adders: faculty (and staff – but not senior administrators) while concurrently lowering costs. Sounds impossible? Over 100 years ago, Frederick Winslow Taylor argued that value-creating organizations can have high wages without suffering from high costs. While wages may increase, other costs go down due to capable people managing and improving great processes. Costs go down because they have consistently high quality and large reductions in re-work, disputes, delays, etc. University leaders need to understand this.

We might also want to think about incentives to help achieve outcomes that would provide even greater value to students. What would happen if full-time faculty and staff received a competitive base pay and benefits, plus profit sharing, as is so often found in the organizations that do Lean well?

This vision, while surely imperfect and in need of the filling-in of many details, outlines how flow in higher education will improve services and reduce costs for a large segment of students. Regardless of the mode of delivery, online or in-classroom, the basic idea is to eliminate waiting and to get information to flow, for the benefit of students [8].

Notes

[1] I do not take as axiomatic that online courses lower costs, either on a unit cost basis or a total cost basis. Online courses (or degree programs) may result in the creation of many new costs for the university (e.g. new support services) or for students (e.g. under-employment) that could make traditional class-room education look inexpensive and also far more valuable.

[2] The level of inattention given to teaching quality and course content by administrators at all levels is astonishing, Yet, this is to be expected when operations management responsibilities are given to people who do not understand operations – e.g. when a humanities professor becomes provost, and is neither given nor takes the initiative to pursue training in operations management and related disciplines (same shit happens in industry all the time, for example when career finance person becomes responsible for operations). An educational institution's life depends on doing good work in the classroom. Yet student evaluations of (full-time) teachers' performance often have little impact on promotion and pay raises, regardless of if performance is exemplary or dreadful. In addition, the senior academic officer is rarely directly involved in assessing teaching performance first-hand (distinct from annual renewal and the promotion and tenure processes). They assume that lower levels of management are appropriately supervising quality, yet with no identifiable process for improvement other than personal motivation to improve one's courses or one's teaching. The provost must frequently communicate directly to students the importance of course evaluations, and that they are taken seriously by university management. Student survey data should be simplified, collected electronically, and the reports generated sent straight to the provost. The senior academic officer should carefully review teaching data for all faculty and departments at least twice per year, together with deans and department chairs (which represents the formal reporting lines to which faculty are accountable). Together, they would assure that faculty teach courses that are their strength, identify those teachers who need help and provide appropriate professional support, and monitor individual teachers' continuous improvement efforts.

Often, the expectation is that established faculty will help their younger peers by volunteering to be faculty mentors. This cheapskate approach introduces enormous variation and is fundamentally inadequate for a professional organization. Provosts must have frequent and direct contact with students, department chairs, and deans to identify teaching process problems – as well as good performance and other opportunities for improvement. The process problems identified would then be the subject of kaizen. In this way, senior university administrators lead efforts to close the gap between their "students are our first priority" rhetoric and the reality that the institution comes first.

[3] Non-profits must, of course, generate profits to return to the business as ongoing investments to fulfill their mission.

[4] N. Modig and P. Åhlström, *This Is Lean*, Limited Review Edition, Rheologica Publishing, Stockholm, Sweden, 2012

[5] Think about this: The cost for a professor to develop a traditional classroom-based course within their knowledge area is perhaps one month of labor, or less than $10,000. The cost to develop an online course with acceptable production values will be multiples of that figure.

[6] M.L. Emiliani, "Using Kaizen to Improve Graduate Business School Degree Programs," *Quality Assurance in Education*, Vol. 13, No. 1, 2005, pp. 37-52

[7] M.L. Emiliani, "Team Leader's Kaizen Manual For Academic Courses and Programs," unpublished work, 2002 (updated 2009, 2012, and 2013).

[8] Contrast this with the for-profit higher education industry. See "For Profit Higher Education: The Failure to Safeguard the Federal Investment and Ensure Student Success," United States Senate Committee on Health, Education, Labor & Pensions, 30 July 2012

Appendix

Additional insights and perspectives on Lean in higher education are contained in five articles previously written by the author. The articles, reprinted here, are:

"How To Get Started With Lean In Higher Ed"
The Lean Professor blog, 7 April 2015

"Lean Must Do No Harm"
The Lean Professor blog, 19 December 2013

"The University As Manufacturer"
The Lean Professor blog, 12 August 2014

"Hire More Faculty,"
The Lean Professor blog, 19 August 2014

"Lean In Higher Education"
First appeared as an online article in February 2005, and later in the book *REAL LEAN: Understanding the Lean Management System* (Volume One), 2007.

I hope you enjoy these articles.

How To Get Started With Lean In Higher Ed

How should higher education (HE) institutions get started with Lean management? Should they follow the tried-and-true path used by for-profit manufacturing and service businesses, or should they create their own new path? Is the rationale for doing the latter sound and also capable of generating improvements in the areas that HE needs it most and at a rate necessary to address strategic challenges?

The vast majority of Lean transformations in industry begin with industrial engineering-based kaizen in the core value-creating processes of a business – the work that matters most to customers. They, after all, must be the first stakeholder that benefits from improvement, while others will follow if kaizen is practiced correctly. Typically, a Lean transformation kicks off with 4 kaizens in operations and one or two kaizens in supporting processes, which the sensei (kaizen teacher) facilitates simultaneously (usually over a 5-day period). Future multi-day kaizens follow a similar pattern.

In industry, kaizen participants learn the goal (flow), the method, the way to think, and practical actions to take. They are encouraged to apply what they learned on a daily basis – daily kaizen – to contribute to rapid improvement in processes. Application of the learning remains focused on improving processes that affect customers – changes that customers can actually see or feel – as well as processes that customers do not see but which are nevertheless important to improve organizational effectiveness.

However, in higher education, the application of Lean principles and practices always begins with non-value-added but necessary administrative work, not core value-creating academic processes such as teaching. If higher education had carefully studied and learned from manufacturing and other service businesses, they would begin with academic processes: teaching, curriculum change process, academic advising, new course development, academic program development, and so on. Perhaps some in higher education did carefully study manufacturing and other service businesses and judged that approach to be unworkable because faculty were resistant to change, would not participate in kaizen, or would not welcome thoughtful scrutiny of their work.

It turns out, faculty are no different than anyone else. Kaizen can be uncomfortable at first, followed by the realization that nearly everyone has: My work can be significantly improved for customers and made much less burdensome on me. Once people realize that kaizen is fun and its outcome is not zero-sum (win-lose), most accept it and say things such as:

- "I was assigned to this kaizen team. I didn't think much of it. I am amazed by what I learned."
- "I would have never believed that could be done if I did not see it with my own eyes."
- "I'm floored by what we accomplished!"
- "This is the fun part of my job."
- "I want to do this every day."
- "I finally see hope."

The different path taken by higher education is significant. After all, the value proposition in higher education for students and payers is teaching and the resultant learning that can be applied to work and to life. Beginning process improvement with non-value-added but necessary administrative work – which typically continues as the sole focus for many years – is not an acceptable response given the many known problems with teaching and their strong effect on reducing student engagement and learning.

So, how does one begin to engage faculty? First, show faculty the need for improvement. Share data with them, such as the data that I have generated: What is Good Quality Teaching?, Are You Satisfied With 10 Percent?, 45 Teaching Errors, The Value of Higher Education, and Higher Education Quality. If your faculty does not like my data, then ask them to quickly replicate these surveys at your college or university. I'd be surprised if the results were markedly different. In addition, it would help to find a faculty member who can explain Lean management and kaizen to your faculty (call on me if you like). Peer-to-peer conversations are often very helpful in overcoming barriers and gaining interest and enthusiasm for kaizen.

Rather than forming a committee to correct teaching problems, go straight to kaizen (not kaizen "event"). The administration (and union) will have to change what counts for faculty's service contribution. Kaizen must count towards service contribution and be weighted more heavily in faculty evaluations than committee work (with the exception of a few very important committees such as those related to undergraduate and graduate curriculum). The learning from kaizen should also be applied to improve committee work processes.

College and universities currently engaged in Lean should re-assess their priorities for process improvement and put greater focus on improving core value-creating processes. Those seeking to transition from conventional management to Lean management should not start out (or remain focused) in areas where improvement will be largely inconsequential from students' and payers' perspectives. They should start in the parts of the university that matter most to students and payers (and employers), so that improvement will be noticed by them which will, in turn, help the university grow and prosper, and assure employment for all – even tenured faculty. The kaizens should be a combination of academic and administrative processes, in a ratio if approximately 4:1.

Finally, please remember that there is no Lean without industrial engineering-based kaizen. Many universities have adopted only simple improvement methods that are the least upsetting to people such as suggestion systems or quality control circles. These are necessary but not sufficient, and the pace of improvement will be slowed by a factor of 100 or more. Do you have 10 years to do a few months worth of improvement?

Nor should universities blindly require everyone to do value stream maps or A3 reports without first understanding what these tools are, who should use them, and under what conditions they are used. Efforts to create value stream maps typically cause large delays in making improvements, while A3 reports, useful for problem-solving and improving critical thinking skills among managers, also delay making improvements. Neither value stream maps nor A3 reports are needed to make major improvements. So, don't get hung up on them. Do kaizen instead.

Lean Must Do No Harm

Progressive Lean management has long been misunderstood and, as a result, misapplied by managers, resulting in bad outcomes for key stakeholders such as employees. Two main points of misunderstanding are: 1) to recognize only the "Continuous Improvement" principle and ignore the "Respect for People principle," and 2) to cherry-pick Lean methods and tools thereby altering the context for their use, impairing their effectiveness, and generating bad outcomes for people. Please, never forget this: It ceases to be Lean management the moment it is used for bad. Lean must do no harm to people – employees, students, payers, communities, suppliers, etc.

Unfortunately, it is difficult for people who are unfamiliar with Lean management to discern the difference between Lean done right and Lean done wrong. Alternatively, people exposed to Lean done wrong quickly formulate negative opinions of Lean that are difficult to overcome. In some cases, people express their dissatisfaction by writing about it, and by doing so they may accurately represent what they have experienced (Lean done wrong), but are not able to describe Lean done right and inadvertently misrepresent Lean management.

What follows is an example from New York City K-12 educational system where team teaching is not working out as planned. This outcome is extrapolated to describe the many ills associated with Lean production and the harm that will likely come to teachers (and the impact on students and parents). These include the six criticisms of progressive management that workers have expressed for over 110 years, and which management usually fails to address: de-humanize them; speed them up and burn them out; de-skill them; take away their knowledge; take away their creativity; and cost them their job. If one or more of these are the actual outcome, then we know for certain that managers misunderstood Lean and practiced it incorrectly.

In the article, "Lean production: Inside the Real War on Public Education" (*Jacobin Magazine*, September 2012, and as re-published in *LaborNotes*, 8 April 2014), the author, Will Johnson, criticizes Lean production. He says this approach to "capitalist production" has as its objective is "to achieve maximum efficiency, management deliberately stresses workplace systems to the point of breakdown." True, if managers ignore the "Respect for People" principle. False, if managers don't ignore the "Respect for People" principle.

He then criticizes important intangibles that are lost as a result of "value-added assessment:"

> "Another hallmark of lean production that's made its way into public schools is value added assessment... In lean schools, value is "specified" as test scores. In a lean school, teachers are managers who supervise the flow of value through their students, whose job is to produce test scores as efficiently as possible. Unless they contribute to the production or flow of value, abstract values like emotional and social development, safety, comfort, and joy are all considered waste."

. If this is actually happening, then school administration is responsible for this terrible outcome. Remember: Lean must do no harm.

Later, Johnson criticizes me by saying:

> "Value added assessments are then used to impose rankings upon teachers. Rankings are another key element of the lean production philosophy. As lean management guru Bob Emiliani puts it, "The final element of... evolving human resource practice was... an annual forced ranking of all associates." Forced rankings will certainly sound familiar to anyone who's been following the recent attacks on teachers from New York to California, where

politicians and media outlets used test-based teacher rankings to publicly humiliate teachers—even when those rankings are statistically meaningless."

Mr. Johnson wrongly suggests that this is my view. Personally, I am a critic of forced ranking processes that do harm, based on my own experience with them. I was describing The Wiremold Company's approach to performance appraisal in the book, *Better Thinking, Better Results* (p. 123), which is not as characterized by Mr. Johnson.

Johnson then says:

"Public humiliation is certainly useful for lean managers who seek to place constant pressure on their employees so that, as Womack and Jones write, they can "do more and more with less and less." The primary goal of forced rankings is, however, to shrink the workforce and see how far remaining workers can be stretched before they crack. Emiliani advises managers to "develop an action plan" for the "bottom ten percent" of workers, and if there's no measurable improvement in performance, "the associate would be subject to involuntary separation." For the best of the workers—more work!"

Mr. Johnson wrongly suggests that it is me who gives such advice to managers. As author of the book, I was describing The Wiremold Company's approach to performance appraisal. Notably, Mr. Johnson ignores the effort that Wiremold managers made to help employees improve their performance so they would not be let go (p. 123). Remember: It ceases to be Lean management the moment it is used for bad. There is no place for public humiliation, for placing constant pressure on employees, for eliminating employees, or stretching employees until hey crack, as these are inconsistent with the "Respect for People principle."

I have no experience in Lean management applied to K-12 education. But people who do tell me that just about everything in *Lean Teaching*, intended for university teachers, applies to K-12 teachers as well. In it, you will find the "Respect for People" principle featured prominently, precisely to avoid the kinds of outcomes that worry both me and Mr. Johnson.

The University As Manufacturer

Most professors do not like to think of the university as business and students as customers, and that higher education is nothing like a manufacturing business. Yet, universities produce a service and provide it to people who pay for the service. It is not a stretch to say that colleges and universities manufacture educational services (just as the auto repair shop in the photo proudly manufactures service). They do this because there is demand from students and payers (either actual or projected).

The process for manufacturing educational services is often poor. So, universities tend to overproduce both courses and degree programs in the hope that some will become popular among students and payers. Overproduction extends to administrative and student support work as well. Over time, universities offer much more than they are capable of delivering with both high quality and low cost.

A funny thing nearly always happens in manufacturing businesses (under US-style management): A steady increase in high-paid overhead administrative positions over time results in high costs that lead to layoffs in operations and the outsourcing of work. In higher education, that means teaching faculty and teaching support staff are affected, while administration continues to grow. It is a remarkable progression of events, given that value is created in operations (teaching), while all other parts of the university and processes support that.

University leaders slowly but steadily begin to forget that teaching, the largest revenue generator – with greatest (often unrealized) profit potential – is what is most important. Their focus turns to survival of the institution, under the guise of "students matter most."

How does this happen? Think about who is looking at costs and making the decisions about where to cut costs. It is the chief financial officer, the provost, the president, and board. First, they conceptualize a simplified version of the academic job as mostly limited to teaching. Next, they recognize the existence of an oversupply of people who are capable of doing the same or very similar work for less. Third, they have an abundance of administrative workers who can be re-assigned to do work that professors once did: academic advising, curriculum development (basically, a purchasing decision), etc.

Full-time teaching will further decline in the near-term in an efforts to help the university survive. Then, 10 or 15 years from now, the errors of this way will be recognized (indeed, obvious), and full-time teaching will return – albeit at reduced levels – just as it has happened with manufacturing.

You may think the university is unlike a manufacturer, but its fate is likely to be the same. Why? Because the chief financial officer, whom the provost, the president, and board place their faith and trust, is blind to distinctions such as manufacturing or service (or higher ed). They see only high costs today and recommend quick ways that will reduce costs tomorrow. Their narrow focus assures similar outcomes across all industries.

But, this fate is avoidable. Progressive leaders of manufacturing businesses, having seen others go down this losing path, see this as an opportunity to prosper. They recognize the "genba (actual place where value-creating work is done) is what's important. Only genba generates profit." But, in order to improve processes on the genba, leaders must think and do things differently than they have in the past – in almost every way. The senior management team bravely adopts Lean management and embarks on efforts to improve every processes in the business, both in operations and administration. Progressive service business leaders do the same.

Are there any brave leaders in higher education?

Hire More Faculty

Why do professors always say, "The administration should hire more faculty"? It seems to be the universal solution to all academic problems that professors face. There are a few sound reasons for this, but some bogus reasons as well.

A sound reason is that adjuncts constitute around 75 percent of the faculty, and full-time faculty only about 25 percent. Part-time faculty cannot (under present structures and rules) fully integrate into department or university affairs, including shared governance. The burden to raise the ranking and reputation of the department, school, or university (through research) – which almost every top administrator wants – falls to ever-smaller numbers of full-time faculty. Often, these faculty are mid-career or later, and may lack the burning fire and fresh, creative mind to do cutting-edge research that younger minds have. They will also cut back on service work ("been there, done that") that younger faculty would gladly participate in. So, the "old-timers" (50+ crowd) focuses on teaching instead, which does little to raise the ranking of a university.

Another reason, one that seems to be quite sound, is enrollment growth. All things being equal, more students means larger classes and less individualized attention to students. So, it makes sense that a department with 25 or 50 new students should hire a new faculty. Or does it? Faculty hiring cannot be in direct proportion to enrollment growth. A department with 25 or 50 new students should not hire one additional faculty, unless there is an unusual circumstance such as the need for a professor with highly specialized knowledge (more on that in a moment).

Taiichi Ohno, the so-called father of Toyota's production system, recounts a story in his book, Toyota Production System (p.69) about hiring in direct proportion to demand. He teaches us that large increases in productive output that are possible, with the addition of only a few more people, when waste, inconsistencies (unevenness), and excesses (unreasonableness) are thoroughly eliminated:

> "Corolla's were fairly popular and selling well. We started with a plan to make 5,000 cars. I instructed the head of the engine section to make 5,000 units and use under 100 workers. After two or three months, he reported, 'We can make 5,000 units with 80 workers.'
>
> After that, the Corolla kept selling well. So I asked him, 'How many workers can make 10,000 units?' He instantly answered, '160 workers.'
>
> So I yelled at him. 'In grade school I was taught that two times eight equals sixteen. After all these years, do you think I should learn that from you? Do you think I'm a fool?'
>
> Before long, 100 workers were making over 10,000 units. We might say that mass production made this possible. But it was due largely to the Toyota production system in which waste, inconsistencies, and excesses were thoroughly eliminated."

Here is the lesson: A department with 200 students should be able to grow to 400 students with the addition of only one or two faculty. But, to do that that requires the thorough elimination of waste, inconsistencies, and excesses in all process that faculty participate in – including those demanded by the administration and accreditors (e.g. reports, reports, and more reports, and committee work, committee work, and more committee work).

Thorough elimination of waste, inconsistencies, and excesses requires two things: Firstly, university leadership that allows departments to totally re-think everything they do and significantly improve all processes via kaizen. Secondly, it requires faculty who are eager to quickly study and improve how they perform administrative work (such as academic advising, academic program assessment, etc.), teaching , research, and service to the department and to the university – and to share with other departments how their new processes work so that their peers can learn from them.

Most universities are an entrepreneurial environment where individual faculty and departments can create new courses and academic programs. However, the processes for creating these new services are poor. So, historically, departments have overproduced both courses and degree programs in the hope that some will become popular among students and payers. Over time, universities offer much more than they are capable of delivering with both high quality and low cost.

As a result of bad management at the highest levels of institutional leadership for long periods of time, a painful effort to reduce and consolidate courses and programs eventually ensues. Hopefully, improved processes (both simple and quick) emerge so that new courses and degree programs are created that serve actual needs (versus politically motivated, such as the recent emphasis on STEM programs). And, that should include improved processes for modifying or shutting down courses and degree programs when demand wanes.

Needless to say, there should be concurrent activity to eliminate waste, inconsistencies, and excesses in administrative processes, including re-deployment of administrators to schools and departments to teach or to support teaching and research.

Another bogus reason for hiring faculty is academic over-specialization. If you owned a business, for-profit or not-for-profit, you would like the people you hire to be multi-skilled so that they can flexibly respond to changing circumstances (e.g. customer demand). You would hire specialists only where they are truly needed.

Universities usually hire single-skilled specialists throughout, and who have limited capability and little interest in doing something else. Faculty hiring practices and promotion processes assure that the university has an inflexible full-time faculty workforce. This, once again, is the result of bad management at the highest levels of institutional leadership for long periods of time.

Even if the administration did hire more faculty, as professors ask, doing so would simply feed existing process problems that are mired in waste, inconsistency, and excess. The only answer, from faculty's perspective, would again be to hire more faculty. That just cannot happen. Nor can the incessant hiring of administrators (at any level) – jobs postings for which typically outpace full-time tenure/tenure track faculty positions by 3.5 to 1 or more.

Lean In Higher Education

The time is right for higher education administrators, faculty, and staff to begin applying Lean management to their business. The consequences of not doing so could be fatal.

Most U.S. colleges and universities face a never-ending struggle to deliver valuable educational services while at the same time maintaining a viable financial position. The normal route for doing both is simply to raise more money from donors and pass cost increases along to customers – not only students – or their parents or the companies that students work for – but also to the companies, state, and federal agencies that fund research.

This inexorable rise in prices, often at rates that greatly exceed the rate of inflation, places unwanted burdens on those who must pay the costs of education and research. This can't go on forever. Surely factors will emerge in the near future that force a change in current pricing practices and value propositions.

University administrators, faculty, and staff have a choice. They can change voluntarily, in an orderly manner while the opportunity exists to do so, or be forced to change when power inevitably shifts to those who pay the bills. Every institution will be affected in some way – even the top-ranked ones – and the shift could occur very rapidly as the cost to deliver information and knowledge drops.

As the population of college-age students begins to decline in some regions of the U.S. after 2010, administrators will face new challenges that they are not yet prepared to address. A likely scenario is:

- Oversupply of capable higher education service providers.
- Degree programs that are not differentiated between competitors.
- Growth of for-profit educational service providers.
- Growth of the distance education market via the Internet.

- Having to compete on the basis of price.

In addition, education standards have become increasingly uniform across the globe, aided by international accreditation bodies such as AACSB International for business schools or ABET for engineering schools [1]. This means that undergraduate engineering or graduate business degree programs in U.S. schools are substantially the same as those offered by schools in Canada or Germany, or by schools in developing nations such as China or Poland (and also taught in English).

If most undergraduate and graduate degree programs are substantially the same, either in reality or perception, then wouldn't most senior corporate executives seek labor that provides the needed capability at the lowest price? Indeed, we are now witnessing the early stages of offshore outsourcing of white-collar "knowledge worker" jobs in information technology, human resources, finance, engineering, law, and medicine. The pace of offshoring white-collar jobs is certain to increase in the coming years and further build the global labor market. In addition to significant job losses, this will also depress the salaries of U.S.-- based knowledge workers who are fortunate to retain their jobs.

If it does not pay to obtain an undergraduate or graduate degree, then some potential students will migrate to jobs that cannot be outsourced offshore such as emergency medical technician, nurse, plumber, carpenter, electrician, hotel and restaurant services, etc. – honorable trades, to be sure. However, enrollment in degree programs will decline more quickly as potential students seek alternatives, and make a bad situation even worse. As a result, some schools will go out of business, some will merge with other schools, and others will exist for a period of time as zombie (half-dead, half-alive) schools.

University administrators, even those at top-tier U.S. schools, should be alarmed because what could happen to higher education is no different than what has already happened to the U.S. steel, electronics, automotive, furniture, and textile industries. And the same thing is now happening to service industries such as customer support, financial analysis, and drug research. While it is true that market dynamics often provide a useful and necessary culling of the weak players, it also offers compelling opportunities to improve and become even stronger.

It seems conditions are forming which could drastically alter the business of higher education as we know it today. Managing through this new phase will be an unpleasant task. So how can institutions willing to face this new reality adapt? One way they can is to do what managers usually do: they lay people off, eliminate programs, cut back on services, close branch campuses, etc. These worn-out solutions will lead to unhappy customers and higher levels of job dissatisfaction among those left to carry out the teaching and provide student services – and could also hasten the school's demise.

Is there a better way to deal with this situation? Of course there is. We need only to reflect on what some managers do when confronted with major upheaval in their industry. They begin to implement Lean management to reduce costs, improve quality, simplify processes, gain market share, stabilize or grow employment, and better satisfy customers.

The question is, will college and university administrators, faculty, and staff wait until the crisis lands upon them, or will they act now to improve?

Professors have written dozens of scholarly papers in recent years illustrating the application of Lean principles and practices to higher education, including: quality function deployment, hoshin kanri, and kaizen. They know there is waste in higher education.

So, there are many people out there who want to improve, and are willing to lead the way. And it's not just faculty. Some administrators and most staff personnel also know there is much room for improving degree programs and related student services. But great ideas are not so great until they are transformed into broad-based action.

Inevitably, however, people in service businesses must overcome the common bias that Lean is a "manufacturing thing," and understand there are many more similarities than differences between manufacturing and service businesses. Administrators, faculty, and staff must avoid the trap of viewing higher education as a special case where Lean does not apply.

People who are not encumbered by mistaken views, and also accept that students are customers – in balance with the purpose of higher education – will want to participate in kaizen to improve individual courses, degree programs, and student services. This will lead to multiple characteristics that clearly differentiate one school from others as seen by customers and lead to positive outcomes.

I think it is relevant to mention my own experience with Lean management in manufacturing and service industries. With the help of extensive training by Shingijutsu consultants in the mid-1990's, we learned and applied Lean management principles and practices in the manufacturing shop and later in supply chains.

Our teams achieved remarkable results, even though our understanding of Lean at that time was somewhat limited by our manufacturing shop floor focus. But we learned many important things about process improvement that laid the foundation for understanding how to improve non-manufacturing processes.

Upon becoming a university professor in the fall of 1999, it was clear to me there was an enormous amount of waste in all facets of higher education – admissions process, advising, individual courses, degree programs, student services, etc. So I did four things:

- Led efforts to reduce confusion and rework by simplifying the school's programs and requirements.
- Conducted seminars for faculty on Lean management and important tools such as root cause analysis.
- Applied Lean principles and practices to the courses I

taught [2] (with great success!).

- Gained the participation of faculty, staff, alumni, and senior managers to improve a graduate M.S. in management degree program using kaizen [3].

The rationale for improvement and related implementation efforts are described in recent papers that I have written (see notes 2 and 3). To make a long story short, Lean principles and practices can be successfully applied to higher education – which should be no surprise. We used improvement processes that were either exactly the same or very close to those long used in industrial manufacturing settings.

Another opportunity is to include Lean principles and practices in all courses – not just in operations management courses. This will result in curricula that teach students how to continuously improve any process and utilize human resources in ways that demonstrate respect for people [4]. It will produce graduates with clearly identifiable value-adding knowledge and capabilities such as creating innovative products or services and improving productivity through fundamental process improvement [5].

Further, students educated in Lean principles and practices – understanding waste, unevenness, and unreasonableness, value stream mapping, kaizen, respect for people, balance, etc. – will be much more highly valued by corporate managers because applying this knowledge leads to better outcomes for all key stakeholders. Plus, it will be harder to outsource their capabilities. And, it will also clearly differentiate the programs offered by some U.S. colleges and universities. But is important to be totally consistent: educators can't just teach Lean principles and practices, they must also apply it to their business.

By the way, another thing that U.S. college and university personnel will have to worry about is non-U.S. institutions of higher education adopting Lean principles and practices first, thus making both their schools and graduates more desirable than U.S. schools and its graduates.

So, the message is: Don't miss this golden opportunity to apply Lean to university management, and also to teach Lean principles and practices to students across a variety of disciplines including arts, sciences, engineering, management, medicine, etc.

You can help by lobbying your alma mater to adopt Lean management.

Notes

[1] Predictably, neither AACSB International (www.aacsb.edu) nor ABET (www.abet.org) suggest or explicitly require educators to teach Lean principles and practices in their respective accreditation standards. This illustrates how obscure Lean is in higher education. Thus, educators have broad leeway to teach concepts, principles, tools, etc., that can maximize waste as well as those that eliminate waste. Unfortunately, teaching people the "least waste way" to think, behave, and work are not yet highly regarded by accreditation bodies. Also, customer demand for this type of education is weak, in part because the value proposition has not been articulated.

[2] M.L. Emiliani, "Improving Business School Courses by Applying Lean Principles and Practices," *Quality Assurance in Education*, Vol. 12, No. 4, 2004, pp. 175-187

[3] M.L. Emiliani, "Using Kaizen to Improve Graduate Business School Degree Programs," *Quality Assurance in Education*, Vol. 13, No. 1, 2005, pp. 37-52

[4] Toyota Motor Corporation, "The Toyota Way 2001," internal document, Toyota City, Japan, April 2001.

[5] M.L. Emiliani, "Is Management Education Beneficial to Society?," *Management Decision*, Vol. 42, No. 3/4, 2004, pp. 481-498

About the Author

M.L. "Bob" Emiliani is a professor in the School of Engineering, Science, and Technology at Connecticut State University in New Britain, Conn., where he teaches courses on Lean management and a unique course that analyzes failures in management decision-making.

Bob holds a bachelor's degree in mechanical engineering from the University of Miami, a master's degree in chemical engineering from the University of Rhode Island, and a Ph.D. degree in Engineering from Brown University.

He worked in the consumer products and aerospace industries for 15 years, beginning as a materials engineer. He has held management positions in engineering, manufacturing, and supply chain management, and had responsibility for implementing Lean in manufacturing and supply chains at Pratt & Whitney.

Bob joined academia in September 1999 at Rensselaer Polytechnic Institute (Hartford, Connecticut campus) and worked there until 2004. He has applied Lean principles and practices to the courses he teaches since he joined academia, and led the first kaizens to improve an accredited master's degree program in 2002-2003. He joined Connecticut State University in 2005.

Emiliani has authored or co-authored 19 books, four book chapters, over 35 peer-reviewed papers on Lean management and related topics, and 10 papers on materials science and engineering. He has received six awards for writing.

Bob served as the North American regional editor for *Supply Chain Management: An International Journal*, 2005-2007 and on the editorial review boards of *Leadership and Organization Development Journal*, 2006-2011, *Supply Chain Management: An International Journal*, 2001-

2011, *Management Decision,* 2001-2011, and *Industrial Marketing Management,* 2005-2009.

He has been an ad-hoc reviewer for *Journal of Management History, Journal of Management Development, International Journal of Operations and Production Management, International Journal of Marketing for Industrial and High Tech Firms, Journal of Marketing Research, International Journal of Electronic Business, and Quality Assurance in Education.*

Please visit my web sites:
- www.leanprofessor.com
- www.profemiliani.net
- www.bobemiliani.com

Made in the USA
Monee, IL
06 October 2022

15359632R00095